ULTIMATE TRIATHLON

PAUL MOORE AND RICHARD HOAD

Note

Whilst every effort has been made to ensure that the content of this book is as technically accurate and as sound as possible, neither the author nor the publishers can accept responsibility for any injury or loss sustained as a result of the use of this material. The publisher has made every effort to secure permission for material used or quoted in this book, however we would be delighted to credit any sources not acknowledged. Ironman® and M-Dot® are registered trademarks of the World Triathlon Coorporation (WTC). For the purposes of readability, we have included the ® symbol only at the first instance.

Published by A&C Black Publishers Ltd
36 Soho Square, London W1D 3QY
www.acblack.com

First edition 2011

Copyright © 2011 Paul Moore and Richard Hoad

ISBN 9781408133163

Acknowledgements
Cover images: Front (top) © Andrew Sawatske; all other cover images © Janick Jenkins

Inside photographs © pp iv, vi, x, 4, 6–8, 11, 15, 19, 20–23, 26, 27, 29–34, 36, 38 (left), 44–45, 47, 51, 55, 56, 59, 62–63, 65–66, 69, 70, 88–89, 93, 100, 104, 107, 109, 111, 112 (right), 113–114, 117–122, 127, 129–131, 133–137, 140 © Janick Jenkins; pp viii, 2–3, 5, 12, 42, 53, 57, 60, 74, 86–87, 90, 97, 116, 126, 132, 135 © Andrew Sawatske; pp 14, 16, 18, 24–25, 35, 37, 49, 52, 64, 67–68, 92, 94–96, 98–99, 102, 105–106, 108, 110, 112 (left) © Shutterstock

Illustrations p 48 © Tom Croft; pp 17, 38–41, 71–73 © Paul Moore and Richard Hoad

Textual design by Steve Russell
Cover design by James Watson

This book is produced using paper that is made from wood grown in managed, sustainable forests. It is natural, renewable and recyclable. The logging and manufacturing processes conform to the environmental regulations of the country of origin.

Typeset in 9pt on 12pt DIN by Saxon Graphics Ltd, Derby, UK

Printed and bound in Singapore by Star Standard

ULTIMATE TRIATHLON

A COMPLETE TRAINING GUIDE FOR LONG-DISTANCE TRIATHLETES

PAUL MOORE AND RICHARD HOAD

>> CONTENTS_

>> FOREWORD_

THE MOMENT I DID my first triathlon I was addicted! I was fascinated by the motivated, energetic and healthy people that I met, not to mention the atmosphere of the race. I wanted to be part of it all!

So I threw myself into swimming, biking and running. Getting fit and being outdoors was so much fun, and I loved feeling that healthy. Over the years I learned there is a great scope for developing within this sport, from short-course to long-distance triathlons (which I focus on today). Through it all I have loved learning about the sport, and I am still learning to this day.

After racing in triathlon for over 15 years my motivation is still very focused on improving my own performance over the three disciplines. I find the challenge of triathlon to be a great motivator – whether that is racing or training – and still enjoy being part of a fun, driven environment. What's more, I continue to meet amazing people in the sport, and those people constantly give me the motivation to keep racing.

I hope you enjoy the triathlon experience as much as I have done. Happy racing!

Bella Bayliss
Fifteen-time Ironman® Champion
(pictured left)

>> INTRODUCTION_

CONGRATULATIONS! IF YOU are reading this, the chances are that you are planning to do a long-distance triathlon, one of the toughest one-day challenges there is. By starting on this journey you are going to experience a rollercoaster of emotions. From the highs to the lows, the tough times to the life changing – memories from this journey will stay with you for the rest of your life.

Sometimes you will be tired and frustrated, sometimes you will experience that rush of pleasure as you see your performances improving and finally, hopefully, you will have that feeling of contentment and joy as you reach the finish line.

This book is designed to take you through the complete process of preparing for – and competing in – a long-distance triathlon. It is structured to guide you through the entire journey, from choosing a race to buying equipment, from designing your training plan to preparing your legs to carry you through the marathon.

And then, of course, there is the race. We cover everything from fuelling to logistics to getting yourself to the finish line. Our goal is to make sure you are fully prepared to take on this challenge, and can maximise your performance on race day.

There is a lot of information to process but the aim of this book is to simplify subjects as much as possible, making them easy to understand and hopefully to execute. You will undoubtedly want to explore some areas in more depth, and we have provided links to further information at the end of the book. Read as much as you can, the more you learn and apply the more successfully you will be able to compete.

Good luck with your training. This is just the start of a hugely rewarding journey that will stay with you for the rest of your life. Enjoy it!

Paul Moore
Richard Hoad

PART 01:
LONG-DISTANCE
TRIATHLON RACES_

>> CHAPTER 001:
THE LONG-DISTANCE TRIATHLON_

'If you set a goal for yourself and are able to achieve it, you have won your race. Your goal can be to come in first, to improve your performance, or just to finish the race – it's up to you.'

– Dave Scott, Triathlete

IN 1977, HAWAII-BASED US Navy Commander John Collins read an article in *Sports Illustrated* that changed the face of triathlon forever. The article was about oxygen uptake, and declared that the Belgian cyclist Eddy Merckx had the highest VO_2max (the maximum amount of oxygen that an individual can utilise during intense exercise) of any athlete ever measured. On the basis of that evidence, Collins concluded that cyclists were the fittest athletes on the planet.

But not everyone agreed with him.

After some debate Collins decided that the only way to settle the dispute was to have a race. He started planning. Looking at already existing events on Oahu, he worked out that they could combine the Waikiki Roughwater Swim (2.4 miles), with a slightly tweaked version of the Around-Oahu Bike Race (112 miles), and finish it off with the Honolulu Marathon (26.2 miles).

The Ironman was born.

Fifteen competitors – and their support teams – started that race on 18 February 1978, twelve finished. John Dunbar, who led off the bike, ran out of water on the marathon (so his support team fed him beer instead), giving Gordon Haller the honour of becoming the first person to earn the moniker of Ironman in a time of 11 hours, 46 minutes and 58 seconds.

Within a few years, the number of competitors had grown dramatically, and in 1981 the organisers switched the race from Oahu to the Big Island. The course has, by-and-large, stayed the same since then. With a swim from Kailua to Kona Bay, an out-and-back bike course that rolls through the incessant heat and wind of the Kona lava fields, and a run from Keauhou back to Keahole Point. The Ironman® World Championship – often referred to simply as Kona – has become the stuff of legends.

It has also proved to be the launch pad for countless similar races. Of course, the single biggest brand in the long-distance triathlon 'market' is Ironman. But Ironman is just one of many brands occupying that space. And while the races may be packaged differently, they all share one abiding truth – they are tough.

Every aspect of long-distance triathlon racing requires a single-minded – almost selfish – dedication to the sport. From simply getting an entry spot in a race (which is becoming as hard as dragging yourself to the start line); to fitting in the weeks and months of gruelling training; from organising the simple logistics of your participation; to maintaining some semblance of balance in your family/work/training schedule: the long-distance triathlon is a physically and mentally challenging journey.

And that's just the preparation; the race itself is something else.

It begins early in the morning with a 2.4-mile (3.8-km) swim. If you assume that the average swimming pool is 25-metres long – that means you have to swim 152 lengths of that pool (with up to 2,000 other people all fighting for position in the water). Once that is done, you have to cycle 112 miles (180km). And when you've finished that, you run for 26.2 miles (42.2km). You have to try to make your legs grind it out, desperately battling a stomach that wants to eject the fuel from your body, and ignoring a brain that is screaming at you to stop.

And that is the long-distance triathlon: a physically, mentally and emotionally challenging journey.

It is a sport that will take you from the highest highs to the lowest lows. It will test your resolve on every level, always pushing you to work harder, be stronger and get faster.

Sounds fun? It is.

Because, however much it hurts, however much that lonely ride in the freezing rain or long run under a searing sun exhausts you, you realise how hard you can push yourself. How far you can go. How tough you actually are. And with that knowledge comes an enormous sense of self-belief and pride.

The journey to completing a long-distance triathlon isn't easy. It isn't meant to be. And it is going to push you, it is going to hurt you, and it is going to make you stronger – both physically and mentally. But when all of the days, weeks and hours finally come together and when you cross that line, you know you have achieved. You have gone further, trained harder, and grown stronger than most of the people on this planet. And there is an indescribable exhilaration that comes with that knowledge.

Not to mention a dull ache in the legs.

>> CHAPTER 002:
CHOOSING YOUR EVENT_

'What we think, or what we know, or what we believe is, in the end, of little
consequence. The only consequence is what we do.'

–John Ruskin, English Author, Art Critic and Social Commentator

IT HAS BEEN said that getting entry to some long-distance triathlons is actually as hard as completing the race itself. And for some of the more famous races that is probably true. But as interest in long-distance triathlon increases, so does the number of races. And while events like Ironman Austria or the Norseman might sell out in a matter of minutes, there are now plenty of events on the calendar that don't demand that you stay up until midnight tapping refresh on your web browser just to get an entry spot.

Because there is such a variety of choice when it comes to racing, what should you actually look for in your long-distance triathlon?

RACE REPUTATION

Although it might not be the first thing you think about, it's always worth trying to find out whether or not a race has a good reputation. After all, you do not want to sacrifice six months of your life (and a lot of money) training for an event, only to turn up and find that the course is sub-standard, the organisation is awful, or the 180km bike involves 10 x 18-km loops!

Before you spend your money, do a bit of research. Make a list of the races that you want to do and then look them up on the internet. Go into triathlon forums, look around on triathlon websites, and just check that there aren't a hundred people talking about how bad the event is. Triathletes are a discerning bunch, and there will, of course, be people who don't like an event. But if there are a lot more negative comments than positive, maybe it's worth considering a different race.

LOCATION

This is a key consideration. There are long-distance triathlons in every corner of the world; from Australia to Brazil and from China to the USA. Where do you want to race? More importantly, where can you afford to race? Remember, if you're racing away from home, you've got a lot of kit, hotels, transfers and food to factor in.

We deal with logistical considerations in Chapter 16, but some initial thoughts to bear in mind when selecting a race are the simple things: do you want to race somewhere warm? Do you want to go somewhere you

haven't been before? Will anyone be able to come along and support you (which is a big consideration when you hit 30km on the marathon)?

Or do you not want to travel at all and incur that extra cost and hassle?

Whichever scenario works best for you, with a bit of research you will (usually) find an event that meets your location criteria.

DATE

The calendar is an important factor in choosing your race. First of all, do you have enough time to train for the event that you have chosen?

If you do, what is the weather like at that time of year? Ideally, you'll select a race that has a nice ambient temperature. However, there are plenty of long-distance triathlons that are run in extreme (usually hot) weather. Do you want to race an event where the average temperature over the past couple of years has been 40°C? Remember that your body needs time to adjust to temperature extremes and you don't want uncontrollable variables ruining your race. The date of the race will also dictate the seasons for when the bulk of your training is going to be. If you don't fancy training over the winter, don't enter an early spring event.

Finally, you need to make sure you can take enough time off work to get to the event, race, and have a day or two to recover afterwards.

IRONMAN OR NOT?

Ironman is a brand. Admittedly, it is a very famous brand, and the name has basically become synonymous with every middle- or long-distance triathlon out there. But there are plenty of other Ironman-distance races in the long-distance triathlon calendar.

For some people, it's all about doing an M-Dot® (the name of the Ironman logo). If you're one of them, then you have 24 (not including the World Championship) very popular races to choose from.

If, however, getting the M-Dot isn't important to you, then have a look around. There is an increasing number of race organisers who boast numerous long-distance triathlons. Some of these races (Challenge Roth and the Norseman, for instance) are as famous and as popular as some of the biggest Ironman events in the world.

COURSE PROFILE

This is a key consideration. Do you want to go fast? Do you want a really, really tough challenge? Or do you just want to complete? Have a look at the course profile and see what the different legs of the race are like.

On paper, some of the information may seem relatively trivial. But if you enter a race with a sea swim, are you used to swimming in salty water? Can you handle waves, for example? On the bike, do you want to tackle some hills? Very few bike courses are completely flat, but some are flatter than others. And on the run, again, do you want to do some hills? How many loops is the run? Remember, you're going to be struggling by this point, so a four-loop run might just send you over the edge...

The unique characteristics of each race should be looked at before you enter so you can meet your personal goals.

IRONMAN BRANDED RACES

The Ironman brand is owned by the World Triathlon Corporation (the WTC) who organise, promote and license the Ironman series of races around the world. There are 24 Ironman races worldwide, each offering qualifying places for the annual Ironman World Championship held in Kona, Hawaii in October.

Qualifying for Kona is an incredible achievement. Each race has a different number of places on offer for Hawaii (between 30 and 65), and the distribution of these places to the various age groups is calculated by the individual race organisers (depending on the number of participants in each age group). As long-distance triathlon grows in popularity, the competition for Kona spots gets fiercer and fiercer. Many of the qualifiers in the most popular age groups (30–34 and 35–39) are semi-professional athletes who spend most of the race competing with the pros. Places are distributed at the awards ceremony the day after the race, and if you have qualified you need to attend the presentation ceremony in person with $550 USD (correct as from 2010) (or local currency equivalent) in cash to pay for your spot.

The 24 Ironman races are listed here in date order (correct as of September 2010).

All Ironman races have their own website, but most of the information that you need for each individual event can be found at www.ironman.com.

Table 2.1 Ironman Calendar 2011

RACE	DATE	LOCATION
Ironman New Zealand	March	Taupo, New Zealand
Ironman South Africa	April	Port Elizabeth, South Africa
Ironman Australia	May	Port Macquarie, Australia
Ironman St George	May	St George, Utah, USA
Ironman Lanzarote Canarias	May	Lanzarote, Canary Islands, Spain
Ironman Texas	May	The Woodlands, Texas, USA
Ironman China	May	Tianjin, China
Ironman Brasil	May	Florianopolis Island, Brazil
Ironman Coeur d'Alene	June	Coeur d'Alene, Idaho, USA
Ironman France	June	Nice, France
Ironman Austria	July	Klagenfurt, Austria
Ironman Switzerland	July	Zurich, Switzerland
Ironman European Championship	July	Frankfurt, Germany
Ironman Lake Placid	July	Lake Placid, New York, USA
Ironman UK	July	Bolton, England
Ironman Regensburg	August	Regensburg, Germany
Ironman Louisville	August	Louisville, Kentucky, USA
Ironman Canada	August	Penticton, British Columbia, Canada
Ironman Wales	September	Pembrokeshire, Wales
Ironman Wisconsin	September	Madison, Wisconsin USA
Ironman World Championship	October	Kona, Hawaii
Ironman Florida	November	Panama City Beach, Florida, USA
Ironman Arizona	November	Tempe, Arizona, USA
Ironman Cozumel	November	Cozumel, Quintana Roo, Mexico
Ironman Western Australia	December	Busselton, Australia

Because Ironman races are, in general, very popular, it is easy to do your homework on them. Forums, websites and magazines all have sections listing the best – and worst – races out there, and it won't take long to find a race that suits you.

NON-IRONMAN BRANDED RACES

Around the world there are numerous long-distance triathlons that are as popular, and sometimes as famous, as Ironman races. A selection is listed below, but a more comprehensive list is kept on the website www.k226.com.

Of particular note are the Challenge Series of long-distance events. Although the jewel in the Challenge crown is Challenge Roth (where long-distance triathlon world records are broken in front of huge crowds), there are also races in Barcelona, Copenhagen, Wanaka in New Zealand and Henley-on-Thames, UK.

Whichever race you decide to enter, just make sure you give yourself enough time to train. Long-distance triathlon racing is tough, even for the professionals. You don't want to turn up on the start line having never swum more than 2km or not knowing what a brick session is. Fortunately, we deal with all of that in the next few chapters.

Right now, though, it's time to commit. Pick a few races, do your homework and then pay your entry fee – it's time to start training!

Table 2.2 A selection of non-Ironman branded races

RACE	DATE	LOCATION	DESCRIPTION
The Forestman	June	Hampshire, England	Long-distance triathlon – much of the run off-road
Challenge Roth	July	Roth, Germany	Long-distance triathlon – known to be one of the world's quickest courses
Outlaw Triathlon	July	Nottingham, England	Long-distance triathlon – new in 2010
Vineman	July	California, USA	Long-distance triathlon – with a smaller number of entrants
Norseman Xtreme	August	Geilo, Norway	Very tough long-distance triathlon – competitors start by jumping into a cold fjord from a ferry at 5 a.m. and finish by running up a mountain
Embrunman	August	Embrun, France	Long-distance triathlon – with a slightly longer bike leg at 188km (with a 5km climb), this is a tough course
Challenge Copenhagen	August	Copenhagen, Denmark	Long-distance triathlon – new in 2010
Elbaman	September	Elba, Italy	Long-distance triathlon – with some climbing on the bike leg
Challenge Barcelona	October	Barcelona, Spain	Very popular event, first run in 2009
Silverman	November	Las Vegas, USA	Another very popular long-distance triathlon
Challenge Wanaka	January	Wanaka, New Zealand	Long-distance triathlon that attracts some of the top athletes

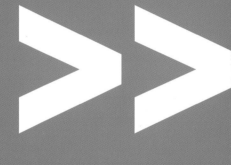

PART 02:
PREPARATION_

>> CHAPTER 003:
EQUIPMENT_

'If you'll not settle for anything less than your best, you will be amazed at what you can accomplish in your lives.'

– Vince Lombardi, Former American Football Coach

BUYING EQUIPMENT FOR long-distance triathlons can be an expensive process. In reality, there really is no limit on the money that you can spend. What's more, triathlon – and more specifically the cycle leg of a triathlon – is one of the few sports where you can actually 'buy' time. If you have the cash to invest there is equipment out there that will save you minutes over the course of a race.

So what should you be buying and where should you get it from? That is where this chapter comes in.

Now, as with the rest of this book, we're going to assume that you have at least a basic understanding of the kit that you need to buy for triathlon. It is also fair to say many of the fundamental principles that guide your purchases for shorter races hold true when it comes to long-distance triathlon, such as shopping around to find the best price, reading reviews of kit before purchasing and trying on before you buy.

MAKING SURE YOUR KIT FITS

There is one golden rule when training and racing at the long-distance: make sure your kit fits. It sounds simple, but it's amazing how many people wear wetsuits that are too small, ride bikes that are too big, or wear running shoes that do nothing to facilitate their gait. Training and racing for long-distance triathlons places a tremendous amount of stress on your body. If you are going to make the physical, social and sheer time investment required for long-distance racing, make sure you don't cut corners on equipment.

WHERE TO BUY YOUR KIT

With the steady growth in the popularity of triathlon, there are more and more shops – both on the high street and online – selling tri-specific equipment. However, one thing that you will notice as you start to

investigate kit purchases is that triathlon equipment is generally not cheap.

There are a few ways around this, the most obvious being to source equipment online. There are a growing number of internet retailers out there who can often undercut shops on price. But for every positive, there is always a negative, and if you buy online you can't guarantee the correct fit.

What's more, triathlon shops are often run – and staffed – by triathletes. And if you have a local tri shop with staff who are friendly, helpful and knowledgeable, they can be a valuable mine of information and advice on equipment and racing in general.

Finally, if you are on a budget then you can always pick up good equipment second-hand. There are countless

online classified and auction sites where you can save a significant amount of money buying anything from running socks to a complete triathlon bike. But before you go down this route you need to know what you are looking to buy.

WHAT TO BUY – THE SWIM

Shopping list: Goggles; tri-suit/tri-shorts; wetsuit

If you've already completed a sprint or standard-distance triathlon, you will probably have this kit already, but if you don't:

Goggles

Given the amount of time you're going to spend in the water, a well fitting, non-leaking, comfortable pair of goggles is an absolute must. There are any number of different styles: from fairly large face-masks to small eye socket-covering race goggles. The main differences in this range are the amount of visibility you have underwater, the quality of the seal against your face and the general comfort level. As these factors are determined by both personal preference and anatomy, it is definitely worth trying a few different models out. On race day you will see all these types of goggles, so it is fair to say there is not one recommendation to go for.

A consideration when buying goggles is whether to buy tinted or clear lenses. Long-distance triathlon races tend to start early in the morning, when the sun is only just rising and low in the sky. With that in mind, tinted lenses can help reduce the glare of the sun and so improve visibility.

Tri-Suit/Tri-Shorts

A serious consideration for all triathletes is whether to change clothing between events. Transition areas usually have dedicated male/female changing areas where you can change in private if you want (nudity is prohibited at triathlon events, so you can't do it in public). Some people do change fully into bike and running gear at each transition, and if you find this is the most comfortable way to race then by all means do it. But you have to consider the time cost. Bearing that in mind, you should seriously consider investing in triathlon-specific clothing, which can be worn throughout the race. Triathlon-specific clothing (whether a single tri-suit or a shorts/top combination) comes in a variety of shapes and sizes and is differentiated from normal sportswear by the shammy. This extra layer of padding protects your nether regions on the bike, and makes the whole experience of triathlon a little more comfortable. It's also quick to dry, avoids chafing and is flexible enough to run in.

It's fair to say that most people wear triathlon-specific clothing on race day. Sometimes competitors choose to wear cycling shorts over their tri-shorts on the bike for added comfort, and some even wear additional shorts for the run.

If you are looking to purchase tri-specific clothing, there are a few things to bear in mind.

1. If wearing a one piece tri-suit, going to the toilet (which is highly likely given the time you're going to spend racing) is going to take a lot longer than normal as you will probably have to unzip the suit and take it off your shoulders down to waist level.

2. A lot of tri-suits do not have pockets in the back. Pockets are invaluable for storing gels, energy bars or general rubbish (some races are very strict on littering), so we recommend you choose a suit with pockets.

3. If you are competing in a race in hot weather, you should look for a top with a long zip to assist in keeping cool (removing your top is not allowed in a

race). A top that has a high level of skin coverage, particularly around the shoulders, can help reduce the chances of sunburn, especially if the material has UV protection as well.

Wetsuit

For most long-distance triathlon events it is compulsory to wear a wetsuit for the swim. However, if you are racing at an event where the water temperature rises above 24°C, the organisers may ban wetsuits altogether, or simply make them optional.

The simple fact is that a wetsuit is a key purchase. Over shorter distances it is feasible to rent one. However, when it comes to long-distance racing, you're going to spend so much time in your wetsuit that it makes sense

to buy one. The good news is that triathlon wetsuits aren't all horrendously expensive.

When determining which wetsuit to buy, there are a dizzying array of brands out there. Some of the most common ones that you will see are: Ironman, Orca, Zoot, 2XU, Sailfish, Blue Seventy, Speedo and Profile. But this is just a random selection. There are plenty more and all of them produce high-quality products.

What you do need to do, however, is get a wetsuit that fits correctly, as outlined in the figure below.

It makes sense to try a wetsuit before you buy. Some shops will – for a small deposit – allow you to test a wetsuit in the water before you buy it. If that is an option, it is one well worth considering. Testing in the

Are there gaps around the shoulders and the crotch? View the wetsuit as a second skin. With that in mind, you need to make sure there isn't too much unused material either under your armpit, around your groin or above the shoulders.

How tight is the seam around the neck? Is it going to let a lot of water in? Water will impact on your buoyancy and ultimately slow you down. The neck seam should be tight but non-restrictive.

Can you extend your arms comfortably? Pretend you are swimming. Does the wetsuit impinge on your arm reach at all? Remember, you're going to be doing a lot of strokes so if you can feel it restricting you after a couple of strokes in a shop, how will it feel after 3.8km?

How long are the arms and legs? Remember, you want to take this thing off quickly. If the arms are right down to your hands it will be much harder to take off in a hurry.

water is, after all, the only safe way of making sure the wetsuit fits you well.

Other Less Essential Items

>> **Swimming cap:** If you are training in cold water, a swimming cap can make a big difference to your comfort. As you will be racing in one, it can also be beneficial to get used to the 'feel' of them.

>> **Anti-chafe stick:** For many people, this is a requirement. Applying wax to the back of your neck, in particular, where the top of the wetsuit rubs the back of your neck, might save you several days of sores. With all the other pain you will be experiencing on race day, an anti-chafe stick can help avoid another one.

>> **Anti-fog for goggles:** If you find your goggles fog up when swimming outside, it might be worth considering buying a bottle of anti-fog to help your visibility.

WHAT TO BUY – THE BIKE RIDE

Shopping list: Bike; helmet; clip-in pedals; cycling shoes; cycling/bib shorts; cycling top; weatherproof layers; cycling gloves; bottle cage; saddle bag; bike pump; track pump; tri-bars.

Whereas some purchases in a standard-distance triathlon are optional, that is not always the case when it comes to long-distance triathlons. You are going to

be cycling an enormous number of miles over the coming months. What's more, it is highly likely that you will be doing your training in various weather conditions. With this in mind, you have to make sure you are equipped to deal with any situation that the elements, the road, or your body throws at you.

So, before we get onto the purchase of the bike itself, let's run through a few of the other essential accessories on your shopping list.

Essential Accessories

>> **Helmet:** This really is a no-brainer. You should be wearing one anyway if you are cycling on the road, and they are obligatory at every triathlon race (regardless of the distance).

>> **Clip-in pedals:** An optional extra that comes highly recommended, clip-in pedals enable you to maximise the performance of the muscles in your legs and so lead to improved speed and efficiency.

>> **Cycling shoes:** Clip-in pedals are useless without the shoes that go with them (the reverse argument applies for clip-in pedals). Just make sure that the cleats you buy match the pedals (there are a few different makes of clip-in pedals). For long-distance triathlon, don't be so concerned with triathlon-specific bike shoes. Instead, focus more on comfort at the expense of the few seconds that might be saved by having just one Velcro strap.

>> **Cycling/bib shorts:** You will be spending so many hours in the saddle that comfort needs to be your first consideration when buying these.

>> **Cycling top:** Cycling tops have pockets on the back, making them invaluable for storing bananas, phones, wallets and inner tubes. They will also wick sweat away from your body and have a long front zip to assist in cooling.

>> **Weatherproof layers:** You don't have to spend the earth (although you can if you want to), but weatherproof layers are crucial. At some point on one of your rides it is going to rain. If you do not have at least a weatherproof jacket to keep your core warm you are going to be cold and miserable.

>> **Cycling gloves:** An optional extra, but they do make cycling more comfortable. Many contain padded gel inserts cushioning the touch points with your handlebars, and they will also protect your hands if you come off.

>> **Bottle cages:** Hydration needs no explanation. The position of your bottles can vary from the standard position on your down tube to cages attached to the back of your saddle or a bottle held between your tri-bars. These latter two options allow you to carry more liquid on a ride and so can be useful additions if you need it.

>> **Saddle bag:** They're relatively cheap and very useful as a place where you can store inner tubes, tyre levers and Allen keys (and sometimes credit cards, phones and cash).

>> **Bike pump:** Usually attached to the bolts on your bottle cages, a bike pump is an absolute necessity. You can either purchase a hand pump, or one that carries CO_2 canisters that inflate your tyre in seconds, potentially saving minutes in a race situation.

>> **Track pump:** It is incredibly difficult to inflate your inner tubes to their optimum psi (between 110 and 140 depending on the tyre) using a hand pump alone. A track pump makes the process very quick and very easy.

The Road Bike

Buying a bike is probably the single most expensive, fun and important purchase that you will make. You are going to spend hundreds of hours and ride thousands of miles sitting on your steed over the coming months, so it is important to make sure you get a bike that:

1. You like (or should that be you love?)

2. Fits properly and is comfortable

You have to use a road bike in pretty much every single long-distance triathlon. If you decide to use a mountain bike or a hybrid bike and are not turned away before the start of the race, be prepared for a very long day in the saddle.

Assuming that you are buying a road bike, it is important to make an honest assessment of both what you can afford and what you will get for your money. You can always find value for money on the internet, and you shouldn't be afraid of buying a bike that is a model from a previous year. But as important as value, is the bike 'fit' itself.

Whether you are buying a road bike for the first time or the tenth time it is always worth getting the bike 'fitted'. This is a service that most (good) bike shops will offer, and it will ensure that your new bike is correctly fitted to your unique body shape. This will help maximise your power output and pedalling efficiency, but also put you in a comfortable riding position.

Of course, you don't have to have your bike fitted on purchase. Plenty of people buy a bike straight off the internet (if they know the size of frame they need), and start training for long-distance triathlon. But back and neck pain is a very real problem for a lot of triathletes, and bike set-up is one of the first things that should be examined if this is a problem that starts to affect you.

Increasing Your Bike Speed

There are three main ways to go faster on your bike. First, you can apply more power to the pedals as a result of all the training you will be putting in over the next few months and which we will come on to in later chapters. Second, reduce the weight of your bike, and third, improve your aerodynamics.

For many of us, the most obvious way to 'buy speed' by decreasing the weight of your bike is upgrading your existing road bike and buying a newer, lighter model. However, riding a bike that is only a few grams lighter will not save you a significant amount of time. If however, you can save a few kilograms of weight, only then might it be worth considering.

For the average triathlete, the bike's aerodynamics matter more than the weight – and that means reducing drag. Drag is caused when something pushes air out of the way so that something can then occupy that space. The shape and the size of that object is important in determining how efficiently air is pushed out of the way and how much air is needed to be pushed out of the way.

There are a number of ways in which a triathlete can reduce drag to increase speed:

>> **Reducing the amount of frontal body area:** The frontal body area is what you can see when someone is riding directly towards you. Simply put, the more frontal area you can see the more drag the rider will be creating and so the harder the rider will have to pedal to overcome the air resistance.

To reduce this frontal area and so the drag created, the majority of long-distance triathletes will use some form of tri-bars, either clipped on to their road bike or as an integrated part of their bars. When using tri-bars, your torso is flatter against the top tube, meaning your frontal area is reduced in size and in turn reduces air resistance.

>> **The aero helmet:** Aero helmets have been proven to offer some of the best- cost vs time-saving ratios compared to other time-saving expenditure. Their teardrop design, with fewer vents provides a more efficient shape for the air to flow across than a standard helmet. If you are committed to reducing as much air resistance as you can (and why wouldn't you be?) and saving every last second, this is an option worth serious consideration.

However, you will find that the majority of long-distance triathlon competitors (although generally not the leading finishers) will not be wearing aero helmets. It is also worth pointing out that Chrissie Wellington (three-time Ironman World Champion) and Craig Alexander (two-time Ironman World Champion) did not wear aero helmets during their victories.

>> **Aero wheels:** Aero wheels are a common sight at long-distance triathlon events, ranging from deep rim wheels to full on disc wheels. There are high entry costs involved with purchasing aero wheels, but there is an associated time saving (and they look good). However, unless money is no obstacle there are cheaper purchases that can prove to be equally time-saving over the course of the race (an aero helmet, for instance).

>> **Wearing tight fitting clothing:** This is a simple point, but loose-fitting clothing flapping in the wind will create more air resistance than tight-fitting clothing. On race day look to wear cycling or tri-specific tops and shorts that fit close to your body. Don't make life harder for yourself unnecessarily!

Tri-Bars

Clip-on tri-bars are the most economical way of cutting down on the drag created by your body. However, road bikes are not necessarily designed for riding in a 'tri' position and you may encounter a number of problems.

When choosing tri-bars there are four main considerations: whether to opt for carbon or alloy (with carbon being lighter but more expensive); how suitable the padding is for your arms; the shape of the tri-bars; and whether the tri-bar is adjustable or not.

The choice comes down to personal preference and what's best for your riding position – although it is recommended that you buy adjustable bars to give you the flexibility of adjustment. A good bike shop will be able to advise on what is best for you.

The key consideration when using tri-bars is being comfortable on the bike. Towards the end of the bike leg of a long-distance triathlon, it isn't uncommon to see age group athletes sitting up and riding on the hoods of their handlebars due to back or shoulder soreness, apparently sacrificing any aerodynamic benefits. If this happens to you, try bringing your saddle position forward to reduce the stretch in your upper body. Also try reducing the drop from the tip of your saddle to the aero bars arm pads using a steeper or adjustable stem. Be careful when making any significant changes to your bike position though, as you might sacrifice power in your quest for being more aerodynamic, creating a net slowing impact instead (the costs of lower power outweighing the benefit of being more aerodynamic). Consulting a qualified bike fitter can help optimise your position.

The Time Trial Bike

You do not need to use a time trial (TT) bike for long-distance triathlons. You will see people using them at events but you will also see a lot of standard road bikes. You will also see a lot of people on standard road bikes posting quicker times than those on TT bikes.

The TT bike is designed to avoid some of the potential problems caused by adding tri-bars to a road bike (hunched neck and shoulder position, stretched lower back, loss of stability in the aero position, a feeling of being cramped and a reduction in breathing efficiency from the sharper angle between thigh and torso) by having a steeper seat tube angle which opens up the gap between the thigh and torso, with the bottom bracket in effect being further back. The top tube on a TT bike is also shorter, reducing the 'stretch' to sit in the aero position. There is also a greater range of positions for the height of the aero bars on the top tube, allowing you to be in a lower, more aerodynamic position if desired.

Access to the gear levers is also easier on the TT bike, with gear levers positioned at the end of the aero bars. This easy access promotes staying in the aero position and using the gears efficiently rather than possibly not shifting because you don't want to keep moving around.

Finally there has been some evidence to suggest athletes run quicker off a TT geometry bike compared to a road geometry bike, as slightly different muscles are engaged during cycling.

There are two main problems with a TT bike. The first and most obvious is the cost. Spending £1.5k plus on a bike like this is a significant investment and not necessarily one that will improve your riding times. The second problem is that TT bikes are designed for racing and time trialling. They are not designed for safe group riding or use in heavy traffic, as access to the brakes takes slightly longer than on a standard road bike. So in buying a TT bike you will be spending a lot of money for a second bike with limited use. TT bikes are really only for the dedicated triathlete.

For your first long-distance race, unless you have the pedigree to suggest a super-fast time or have the equipment from your previous triathlons, spending extra thousands of pounds is certainly not necessary. It's better to have a decent bike, an excellent riding position and then complete a lot of high-quality training. Adding on all the bells and whistles might offer more value if you have a taste for triathlon that extends beyond just a handful of races. However, when you get to the transition area and see some of the kit on display, it's easy to get very slightly envious!

WHAT TO BUY – THE RUN

Shopping list: Shoes; hydration system

Shoes

One of the most important purchases that you will make for your long-distance training and racing is properly fitting running shoes. It is worth taking time and investing money in the right pair as they can, quite literally, mean the difference between finishing the race and finishing your career as a triathlete.

A person's running style varies dramatically, but the running shoe market is well developed and offer a shoe for most styles. To determine which is the correct pair of running shoes for you, it is advisable to go to a running – or triathlon – shop which offers gait analysis. This is a facility that will measure how – and where – your foot strikes the ground, how your ankles and legs respond to that strike, and so work out what is the best type of shoe for you.

When you are having your gait analysed, you will find attendants referring to three different types of running style.

>> **Neutral pronation:** As the outside of the heel hits the ground, the foot rolls in evenly without any adverse affects. When you push off the ground, you do so evenly. This is the effective distribution of weight and is neutral (or normal) pronation.

>> **Over-pronation:** When the heel strikes the ground, your ankle and lower leg rolls inwards, putting a lot of weight on your big toe. When you push off, you do so on the inside of your feet. This is common in people with low foot arches.

>> **Under-pronation (or supination):** The opposite of over-pronation, your ankle does not roll in enough when your heel hits the ground. Your weight is on the outside of the foot. This is common in people with high foot arches.

By purchasing a pair of running shoes that compensates for any imbalances in your running style (or simply complements your neutral pronation) you will dramatically reduce the risk of injury and so have a more enjoyable running experience.

Remember: you are training for a marathon. That's a lot of training and a lot of racing. Invest in shoes that work well with your running style, and your legs will carry you to the end (provided that you do the training).

Hydration System

On your long runs you will need to take some fluids with you. Apart from the obvious method of carrying a plastic bottle with you, there are also several hands-free options. There are numerous backpacks that have integrated hydration systems, and there are also waist belts that allow you to attach hydration to them. Both the backpack and the waist belt also allow you to store nutrition, money and keys.

Most good running or triathlon shops will have a range of these products. Have a look at them and see what works for you.

>> CHAPTER 004:
DEFINING AND MANAGING THE
TRAINING PLAN_

'Don't dilute your feelings of success and accomplishment on race day by setting unrealistic goals.'

– James Cunnama, Ironman Champion

THROUGHOUT THE COURSE of this book you'll hear numerous references to things that are essential in getting you to the finish line of your first long-distance triathlon, or improving your time for future races. And while every single one of them is key, defining – and managing – a successful training plan is one of the most important things that you can do.

Your training plan is going to govern what you do and when. Obviously you don't have to stick to it resolutely. It is, after all, little more than a series of guidelines that don't take into account injuries, fatigue or changing external commitments. But that's why you need to approach your training plan rationally. If you manage and maintain it, then you can use it to motivate yourself, and it will become the central piece of your long-distance triathlon jigsaw.

For most people, the biggest challenge of pulling together a training plan comes from knowing what to do and when. Some will go ballistic from the off, others will build progressively. Speak to any professional, and they will tell you that the athletes who fall into the latter category will have a more positive long-distance triathlon experience because they will avoid burnout.

Burnout (both mental and physical) is a common barrier to the completion of a long-distance triathlon, and is a real danger in the weeks and months leading up to the race. Burnout is discussed in Chapter 15.

THE TRAINING PLAN

Your training plan has to be dictated by reality. How many months do you have until race day? How many hours a week can you train? What are your external commitments? Be realistic from the outset, otherwise you will start missing goals, which can impact on motivation.

For the purposes of this book, we are working on the premise that you have 24 weeks before your first long-distance triathlon. We've used 24 weeks because this should be enough time for people with an existing fitness base to build up the necessary endurance to complete the race. In this instance 'existing fitness base' means you've done triathlons before (whether standard- or middle-distance events), and you can swim, bike and run competently. Obviously the fitter you are at the start of the training period – or the bigger your endurance base – the better your result should be

at the end of the training plan. However, having a smooth 24-week build-up is rare (and fortunate), so keep focused on what you are trying to achieve and stay motivated towards that goal.

The 24-week plan is divided into four distinct phases as follows:

>> Base phase (ten weeks): The purpose of this phase is to put down some core fitness and establish your endurance base. It is characterised by low intensity training for the bike and run, slower efforts that gradually build in length. For the swim this phase is focused on improving technique and swim speed before adding endurance later. The base phase is also concerned with general preparation, getting your diet right, ensuring you have the right equipment and getting yourself into the routine of consistent training.

>> Build phase (ten weeks): In this second phase, you should introduce some more quality training and start to get your body used to race pace. We recommend that you do some short and even middle-distance racing for practice, for getting the feel of a race event and as a trial run for your kit and your nutrition strategy. For beginners, who are still developing their endurance base, this phase should be treated as an extension to the base phase and used to continue to develop your ability to complete the distance.

>> Peak phase (three weeks): In this phase you can wind down the long training effort and include some

shorter, faster sessions to get your body primed to peak on race day. The main consideration in this phase is to ensure your legs are feeling fresh, you are getting enough rest, eating and drinking enough and are fully prepared for race day from a practical point of view. The gradual reduction in volume and intensity of training before the race is known as the taper (see Chapter 12).

>> **Race week (one week):** There are no fitness gains to be had in this week. Sessions are light and short, intended to keep your body feeling good and your mind sharp. Practical considerations around travelling to the event are likely to dominate the week.

Working through these phases will help your body (and mind) become accustomed to the demands of long-

distance triathlon. Your body will gradually get used to dealing with long sessions, and then as these longer sessions become interspersed with race pace and slightly faster training, you manage your training to help you peak at the right time.

As well as the training plan example we have included in Chapter 11, there are other plans you can find on the internet for free (or at a cost), and you can even get yourself a personalised coach if you have the money and inclination.

What we would recommend, though, is to read as much as possible and if you can, talk to people who have done long-distance racing before. If nothing else you may learn from their training mistakes, which can be invaluable knowledge as your training progresses.

In tandem with the plan should be your training diary, which records what you've done, how you felt and lessons learned. As well as being a useful tool if you ever do another long-distance race, it's great to look back at the hard work you've put in before race day and can be good for mentally preparing yourself.

THE IMPORTANCE OF REST AND THE RISK OF BURNOUT

Putting in week after week of training without recovery periods is not the way to optimise your training potential. As you've probably heard on many occasions, taking time to rest and recover is as important as the training itself, allowing the body to benefit from the hard training it has previously endured.

The 24-week programme works in cycles of two hard weeks followed by a very easy third week. The hard weeks also incorporate some easier days. If this is still too much, think about incorporating additional 'easy' days into the harder two weeks, or simply reduce the cycle to ten days of hard training followed by five of easier training.

Only *you* can determine how much and how often you need to rest. Your body will give you signs when it needs to rest: you will feel constantly lethargic; your heart rate will shoot through the roof on a standard session; you might feel physically exhausted. All of this can be remedied by rest and a rational review of your training plan.

On top of physical exhaustion, it is not uncommon for long-distance triathletes to experience periods of psychological stress; of thinking that their training is not going to plan or that they simply have not done enough. Some of the most common thoughts are listed below:

>> 'I haven't done enough training'

It's natural to have moments like this, and everyone has them. But if you have been sticking to the majority of your training plan sessions (particularly the longer-distance efforts) you will have done enough to get across the line. In a race like a long-distance triathlon, it is very rare for either novice athletes or seasoned veterans to stand on the start line and be completely happy with the amount of training that they have done.

>> 'My training bike splits are slow despite the fact I thought I was a faster cyclist'

The simple fact is that when you head out on those long rides, you are dealing with a whole lot of variables that are not going to come into play on race day: traffic lights, other road users, junctions etc. Your ride on race day will be a completely different experience. If you need to give yourself a little boost, though, a middle-distance triathlon or a cycle sportive can give you a good indicator of your potential triathlon speed. A lot of athletes cycle a lot faster in a race than they have ever done during a training ride.

>> 'I find brick sessions really tough. How am I going to do this marathon?'

Brick sessions are tough, but they can be really useful in getting you ready for a race. Make no mistake – the marathon will be really hard. You need to be ready mentally to deal with any low points

you may have. Walk when you have to, but try and not walk all the time, ensure you are taking on enough fuel, keep a positive outlook and keep pushing yourself. Do your endurance runs in training and use this time to visualise how you will react on race day. Everyone is hurting – it's how you deal with it that makes the difference.

>> 'I'm struggling with motivation'

Take the physical strain of all the training and couple that with dealing with real life and you have a recipe for motivational meltdown. It happens to everyone, particularly athletes with a longer build-up to race day. There are four ways to deal with this:

1. Give yourself a few days off. Forget about training and racing altogether and go and do something fun.

2. Try some different routes or find some training partners. Having people to cycle or run with can really boost motivation.

3. Target smaller goals. Scott Neyedli, one of the UK's top long-distance athletes, believes this is essential for age group athletes: 'I think it's important to have some sort of target race or main goal at the end of each month. It doesn't have to be a race. It could be a time-trial in the pool or on the bike, doing a half-marathon in a certain time, even weight-orientated towards the summer.'

4. Look at your reasons for doing a long-distance triathlon. Write them down and revisit them when you are struggling for motivation. You are on the road to achieving something significant here – just keep focused on your goal.

>> 'I'm injured and I can't train'

Rushing yourself back from injury is an easy way to exacerbate existing problems. It takes real discipline to slowly (but correctly) build back up again. It may be that you will have to reassess your goals following

a serious injury, but if you are out for just a few weeks the situation is salvageable (sometimes a short-term injury and the enforced rest can be of benefit).

Physical fatigue and mental self-doubt are common among long-distance triathletes. However, beyond the expected levels of fatigue lies burnout. Burnout (both mental and physical) is a common barrier to the completion of a long-distance triathlon, and is a real danger in the weeks and months leading up to the race. If you feel utterly exhausted all the time (despite resting), take zero enjoyment from what you are doing, or just feel a bit broken, it may well be that you are burnt out. We offer advice on dealing with burnout in Chapter 15.

ONE LAST TIME: DON'T BE A SLAVE

We've said it before, but we're going to say it again: your training plan is not the be-all and end-all. You need to be pragmatic in your approach to training, and accept that often life simply gets in the way. Keeping the plan dynamic and ensuring that you are constantly working on your weaknesses and maintaining your strengths is a vital element to your development. Do not consider the plan to be a static document, but one that evolves as you learn more about your strengths and weaknesses and begin to develop your own fitness. Never forget that the end goal is how you perform on race day, ensure your training plan sets you up for this day.

>> CHAPTER 005:
TRAINING INTENSITIES_

'I hated every minute of training, but I said, "Don't quit. Suffer now and live the rest of your life as a champion."'

– Muhammad Ali, Former Boxer

ESTABLISHING YOUR TRAINING AND RACE PACE

Understanding how to pace yourself is a crucial element of your training plan. If you go out pushing hard sessions every day, you will end up exhausting and possibly injuring yourself. You will also unlikely complete the necessary volume of training required to build up your endurance base.

Much of your training will be at a low level of intensity, building your aerobic endurance base. Aerobic exercise is when glycogen is broken down to produce glucose, which then reacts with oxygen to produce water and carbon dioxide and release energy. When you run out of carbohydrates the body starts to eat into the fat reserves, which are a lot less efficient at releasing energy. This is when endurance athletes typically 'hit

the wall'. During anaerobic exercise, glycogen or sugar is used without oxygen and is much less efficient, designed for short bursts of energy usage such as sprinting.

With a strong aerobic base of fitness your body will become efficient at generating energy helping to develop the slow twitch muscles you need to keep going for such a long period of time. Maintaining the right intensity levels in training will not only develop these attributes but also allow you to complete the number and length of sessions required to train for a long-distance triathlon. In fact, one of the keys to success in your race is to keep a consistent level of training going during your training period. This consistency can only be achieved by keeping check on the intensity at which you are training. Keep training too hard and you will risk exhaustion and possibly compromise your end goal.

How do you train at the right level of intensity? One of the best ways to manage this is to use a heart rate monitor. Over time, this will help you develop an understanding of your body's levels of exertion, allowing you to judge perceived effort. Another useful tool, for the bike ride, is a power meter, which uses the amount of wattage produced as an indicator of training effort. If you are keen to develop and understand your cycling performance this is a worthwhile purchase, although beyond the scope of this book (there are plenty of books and websites which provide detail on using a power meter).

The Heart Rate Monitor

Using a heart rate monitor is not a necessity, but it can be an excellent way of controlling your training and racing efforts. There are numerous heart rate monitors in the shops, although there are two or three brands that dominate the market. As with everything in triathlon, you can spend a lot of money on this kind of equipment, but a basic model will often do everything you really need it to. Many models now incorporate a GPS system into the watch that will tell you how far you've gone and how quickly you are going, which can be useful for your run and bike training. This extra functionality can be costly so again it's worth thinking about exactly what you need before spending lots of money.

For the purposes of this section, however, all we are interested in is the basic heart rate monitor and how to use it effectively.

The science behind heart rate monitors is quite complex, and if you really want to delve into it, there's plenty to find out. However, you don't have to be an expert to get the most out of your heart rate monitor. What you do need to do, though, is establish two things: your resting heart rate and your maximum heart rate.

The former is pretty easy. Your heart is usually at its most rested during sleep, and if you measure your heart rate a few minutes after you wake up (your heart rate is often slightly higher immediately after waking so give it some time to settle) you'll get a pretty accurate reading, especially if you take a sample over several days to avoid any adverse readings.

Your maximum heart rate requires a little more effort to measure. Without going for proper tests, there are a few ways to determine your maximum heart rate, one of which is as follows. After a good warm-up, run as hard as you can for two minutes, then jog for a minute, then run as hard as you can for another two minutes. Your heart rate in this second period will be something close to your maximum.

By determining your maximum and minimum heart rates, you can start to develop a training plan that incorporates training in the optimum 'zones'.

This is where the science of the sport comes in. Your body responds to the zones that your heart rate operates in, and that in turn dictates both how long you can train for and how quickly you will recover.

With that in mind, all of your training sessions should be governed by heart rate 'zones'. These are your heart rate levels during exercise, and can be split into four major categories:

1. Recovery (less than 70 per cent of your maximum heart rate). This is effectively the warm-down period of your training but still develops your aerobic capacity and endurance.

2. Endurance (between 70 and 80 per cent of your maximum heart rate). You will get the maximum aerobic benefit out of these sessions, and they are essential to your long-distance triathlon development. Most of your running and long rides will be in the lower part of this zone as your endurance increases and cardiovascular efficiency improves.

3. Tempo (between 80 and 90 per cent of your maximum heart rate). In this zone your body will predominantly use glycogen as an energy source. One of the by-products of this is the production of lactic acid, which at a certain level of intensity will stop being cleared from your muscles and will quickly impact on your performance. This point is known as your anaerobic threshold (AT). During your long-distance race you should never be going hard enough to reach your AT. Improving this threshold will come as the result of a stronger aerobic base and some training in the tempo zone.

4. Max (above 90 per cent of your maximum heart rate). You will hardly ever be in this zone for your training, perhaps only for some high-intensity swimming sessions.

Once you have established your maximum and resting heart rate, you can determine what heart rate equates to which of the four zones. The easiest method is to employ the following formula:

(max HR – min HR) x per cent as a decimal + min HR. For example to find 75 per cent of max with 190 max and 50 min: 190 – 50 = 140 x 0.75 = 105 + 50 = 155.

With this in mind, someone with a maximum heart rate of 190bpm and a minimum heart rate of 50bpm would have a recovery heart rate of a maximum of 148bpm, an endurance heart rate of a maximum of 162bpm, a tempo heart rate of a maximum of 176bpm

and a max training heart rate (say, 95 per cent) of 183bpm.

As we have already said, most of your training in the early stages of your preparation for the bike and run will occur in the endurance zone, allowing you to build the volume and distance of training without getting exhausted. As your endurance base develops some higher intensity elements are included. For the swim a lot of your training will involve swimming intervals and so will be more often in the tempo zone.

If you are not keen on using a heart rate monitor then another option is to use a measure of 'perceived effort' that matches heart rate exertion levels. Perceived effort is a subjective measure, using how you are feeling to equate to controlling your pace. While in no way scientific it can work as a substitute to using a heart rate monitor.

Table 5.1 Levels of Perceived Effort

LEVEL	PERCEIVED EFFORT	PACE	HOW IT FEELS
1	45%	Easy	Used for recovery, feels comfortable, can easily hold a conversation
2	45–65%	Steady	Rhythmic running/cycling, swimming, can sustain for long distances
3	65–85%	Stretched	Feels hard but controlled, not at maximum effort
4	85–100%	Fast	As hard as you can go for the distance

The above levels are included in the training programme as a general guide to how hard you should be working in each training session.

CHAPTER 006:
WARMING UP, WARMING DOWN
AND STRETCHING_

'If you spend too much time warming up, you'll miss the race. If you don't warm-up at all, you may not finish the race.'

– Grand Heidrich, Athlete

WARMING UP, WARMING down and stretching will help you get the most out of your training programme through preparing your body for exercise, optimising your recovery from exercise, reducing the likelihood of injury and improving your general flexibility. While they are easy elements to skip, they will maximise the effectiveness of your training and so are worth completing.

WARMING UP

During the early stages of a training session, a warm-up and stretching session is essential. As well as providing your muscles with the heat, elasticity and bounce required to do what you want them to do, a warm-up also releases lubrication from the cartilage that gives the muscles increased flexibility and stops bones from grating. Added to that, a gentle warm-up facilitates a more effective flow of blood, and helps the cardiovascular and respiratory systems prepare for stress.

WARMING DOWN

Warming down is just as important as warming up, as it helps your body return to its resting state. During a warm-down you should be exercising at perceived effort level one, and should feel your cardiovascular, respiratory and muscular systems gradually returning to their normal functioning.

STRETCHING

Stretching will improve your flexibility and prepare the muscles for exercise or aid recovery following a training session. Good flexibility is important for the long-distance triathlete, helping to improve technique, maintain form for a longer period and maximise the range of movement in your stroke, stride or pedal revolution.

So how and what should you stretch? Well, the key is to make sure you stretch all of the major muscle groups

for the particular exercise you have done or are about to do. To give you an idea:

>> **Swimming:** Abdominals, biceps, triceps, shoulders, glutes, hamstrings

>> **Cycling:** Glutes, thighs, hamstrings, calves

>> **Running:** Glutes, thighs, hamstrings, calves, abdominals, tibialis anterior (on the front of your leg)

Stretching can be dynamic, using a range of motions while active, for example arm rotations, heel kicks, high knees and skips, or static. Static stretching happens in a more controlled stationary manner.

WARM-UP STRETCHING

Stretching following a warm-up has a different purpose to stretching following a warm-down. Elasticity is the key in a warm-up, and you're trying to get the spring in your muscles so you feel loose and ready. With that in mind:

>> Stretching for the run should involve a mix of dynamic and static stretching. Dynamic stretching could include rotational arms, heel kicks, high knees, skips, strides, quick feet, knee drives and foot flicks. Static stretching is demonstrated later in this chapter.

>> Stretching for the bike will generally be static following a good warm-up of spinning.

>> Stretching for the swim is likely to be a mix of drills and static stretching.

>> For stretches:

>> Do not hold the stretch for too long; 10–20 seconds should be enough.

>> Do not overstretch. Push to what feels comfortable.

>> Do not bounce into the stretch; extend in a slow and controlled way.

>> Repeat a stretch between three and five times and complete 2–3 sets.

WARM-DOWN STRETCHING

For stretching following a warm-down, instead of trying to achieve elasticity and bounce, now your goal is to maintain flexibility and expedite recovery.

The basic principles of warm-down stretching are:

>> Stretches are held for longer. A minimum stretch should be held for at least 30 seconds, but no more than a minute.

>> It is important to push the stretch. Spend ten seconds at a comfortable stretch, then try and go a little lower or push a little harder for the next ten seconds, and then do the same for the third ten seconds. The goal is to elongate the muscles. It is important to be sensible though. If something feels really uncomfortable, the chances are it isn't doing you much good.

Repeat each set a minimum of 3–5 times.

Below are some of the key static stretches you could include in your stretching routine. Needless to say, there are a large number of alternatives and a physiotherapist can provide you with a tailor-made stretching routine if you wish to do something a little more structured. If not, this will certainly suffice.

SWIM STRETCHES

Shoulders/upper chest

1. Lock your fingers together with palms facing outwards. Lift above your head feeling the stretch in your shoulders and upper chest.

2. Take one arm over your head so your palm is touching your upper spine. Using the other hand push gently down on the elbow. You should feel the stretch in the shoulder.

3. Put your arms behind you with fingers interlocking. Raise your arms upwards, feeling the stretch in your lower shoulders.

Lats

1. Start with your hands flat, one in front of the other with fingers touching. Reach up with your hands above your head and arms straight. Keeping your legs and waist still, lean your hands over to the right-hand side, repeat for the left-hand side.

LEG STRETCHES

Hamstrings/back

1. Keeping your legs straight, reach down slowly to your toes with your fingertips until you can feel a gentle pull. Never push down further than what feels comfortable and don't bounce on the stretch, move slowly down and up.

4. Keeping your arm straight spin it slowly around in a full circle, repeat three times forward and three times backwards and then change arms.

Chest muscles

1. Have your torso perpendicular to the wall and your feet parallel to it. Reach your arm back with palm outstretched facing the wall. You should feel the stretch in your shoulder and upper chest.

2. Sit on the ground with one leg out straight and the other bent in with the sole of the foot touching your inner thigh. Stretch for your toes with right arm going to right leg, feeling the stretch in your hamstring.

Quads

1. Pull your foot towards your buttocks, keeping your upper body straight and in line with your upper leg. Feel the stretch in your quad.

Calf/Achilles

1. Lean against a wall with the palms of your hands, keeping one of your legs straight and stretched out behind you. Gently push forward, stretching out the back of your straightened leg. Bending the knee of the straightened leg will stretch the Achilles.

2. Keep your front leg straight and rear leg slightly bent. Feel the stretch in the calf and Achilles of your rear leg.

Illio-tibial band (ITB)

1. Lie on your back, put your right ankle on the opposite knee. Put your right hand on the inside of the knee, putting pressure to feel the stretch on the outside of the thigh/hip. Repeat with the other leg.

2. Sit down crossing the right leg over the left. Put your left arm down the outside of the crossed leg and push, twisting the body in the opposite direction to the leg. The stretch should be felt down the outside of the right thigh.

Inner thigh

1. Sit on the floor with your legs apart and the soles of your feet touching. Using your elbows, push the inside of your knees towards the ground, feeling the stretch in your inner thigh area.

**PART 03:
TRAINING_**

>> CHAPTER 007:
SWIM TRAINING_

'It doesn't matter how many kilometres in the pool you do, you're still not going to swim quicker than someone who has a better technique.'

– Pete Jacobs, Professional Triathlete

EVERY TRIATHLON SWIM is a full-on contact sport. As soon as the gun goes off, the water is transformed into a heaving mass of flailing limbs, with every athlete aiming for a single buoy in the distance. The experience can be quite overwhelming. As competitor after competitor pummels their way towards that buoy – and you find yourself gasping for every ounce of air and reaching for every spot of free space available – there might be times when you want to quit. When you want to flip over onto your back or simply turn around and head for shore.

But that wouldn't do justice to the amount of work and effort you've put into your swim. And getting the long-distance triathlon swim 'right' takes effort. What's more, it takes hours of dedication.

Not to mention a carefully crafted training plan.

Because training for the 3.8-km swim is tough. Most people haven't swum 3.8km before they enter a long-distance race (a lot of people haven't even done half of that). So what do they do? They start to slog. They grind it out (a common approach to long-distance training).

They go backwards and forwards, each week inching a little bit closer to the fabled 4-km mark (after all, if you're swimming 3.8km you might as well train to 4km and give yourself a bit of extra confidence). They do eventually get there. But in the process a lot of people get very bored or even disillusioned with swimming. And most people who approach training like this find it impossible to swim any faster.

Sure, they can swim further. But triathletes in training often find that they do a 1,500m time-trial more slowly after regularly swimming 4km. Why? Because if you train at one (usually slower) speed over a greater distance then that is all your body will know how to do. And so it will slow down. The goal of your swim training should, of course, be to comfortably swim 3.8km. But you must be careful that your extra distance training does not come at the cost of losing speed. What you really want is to swim faster than ever.

To get the right perspective on this, let's look at how fast triathletes swim at long-distance triathlon races.

Table 7.1: Ranked Swim Times For Four Long-Distance Triathlons 2010

SWIM	IRONMAN AUSTRIA	QUELLE ROTH	IRONMAN UK	NORSEMAN
Mins/Secs				
<10	48.02	50.44	48.48	59.00
<100	58.02	57.03	58.29	76.00
<500	66.28	64.31	71.59	–
<1,000	72.3	69.5	89.47	–
<1,500	79.28	74.32	–	–
<2,000	90.56	80.13	–	–
Last Place	143.23	123.32	134.14	128.00

The table above sets out swim times by rankings for four long-distance triathlons raced in 2010, all with a swim distance of 3.8km. So, for example, the tenth best swim time in Challenge Roth in 2010 was 50 minutes and 44 seconds. The 2000th best swim time in Ironman Austria was 90 minutes 56 seconds.

Remember these athletes were wearing wetsuits, swimming in open water, many with the benefits of drafting (see page 51) but also with the disadvantage of getting bashed by hundreds of other swimmers.

What does this tell us about the quality of swimming at these long-distance triathlons? Well, first and most is obviously is that the fastest swimmers are extraordinarily quick. To get in the top ten best swim times you would need to swim 48 minutes in Austria and the UK, approximately 2½ minutes per 200m. Try this in your local pool and you will get an idea of how quick it is. This speed isn't confined to the professional men either; the leading women often swim at the same speed as the leading men in long-distance races.

Away from the faster swimmers, the most important thing to note is the range of swim times produced. The slowest swimmer in Austria came in over 90 minutes behind the fastest (although in this case missing the 2 hour 20 minute cut-off time). As long as you can hit the cut-off point there will always be a number of people surrounding you.

The final point to note is that swim courses vary and so times will vary, based on variables like currents, wind or how the course deals with up to 2,000 people swimming at the same time. The Norseman, for example, starts in a cold fjord and is susceptible to adverse currents, which can result in a more challenging swim and therefore potentially much slower swim times.

SWIM BASICS

For the purposes of this chapter we are going to assume that you already know the basics of front crawl. What's more, we are going to assume that you have taken part in a triathlon (or at least an open-water swimming event). If you haven't, you might want to do that before you try your hand at the long-distance triathlon swim.

Of course, we're not saying that you should have the perfect swimming technique, but you should be able to swim 1,500m comfortably and, ideally, you should be able to do it front crawl. As with any triathlon event, you can complete the swimming leg of the long-distance triathlon using the stroke of your choice, but front crawl is the quickest and most efficient stroke, and 99 per cent of people go down that route.

When front crawl is executed correctly around 80 per cent of the forward propulsion comes from the upper body. However, a quick visit to your local pool will be enough to convince you that in a lot of cases front crawl

is done anything other than correctly. It's not uncommon to see people thrashing about, their legs acting like anchors as they desperately try to propel themselves through the water. Compare them to people who swim 'well'. You know the ones: they make it look effortless. There's no splash, their bodies slip easily through the water and they're fast.

To be that good often takes years of training (and that won't be enough for many of us). And the reason they find swimming 'easy' is because somebody, somewhere has drilled technique into them. It probably happened when they were kids, and now their bodies do it naturally. But they are that good because they have good technique.

Sure, upper body strength plays a part in the swim. But technique is far more important. Take the 2009 Ironman World Championship, for example. Craig

Alexander (the eventual winner of the men's race) came out of the water in 50:57. Interestingly, the first woman out of the water was hot on his heels (50:58). That demonstrates again that technique is more important than just raw strength.

Pete Jacobs is another case in point. One of the fastest swimmers in long-distance triathlons, Pete sometimes swims just 5km in a week. Why is he so quick? Because his technique is close to flawless. What's more, every time he gets in the pool he is trying to hone his technique more and more (making him faster and faster). As Pete said in an interview, 'With less training I'm going quicker just because I'm thinking more about technique.'

So what should you be looking for when it comes to technique?

The key fundamentals to a good front crawl stroke are listed below:

>> Have a good body roll. As one arm is lifted out of the water the body should roll in the same motion. It does not help if your arms are windmilling on the side of a flat body. Rotation makes your body more streamlined in the water, lowering your drag and increasing your speed.

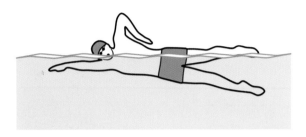

>> Breathe bilaterally (i.e. on both sides). Bilateral breathing helps develop your body roll and keeps the stroke symmetrical. You don't have to breathe bilaterally all the time, but doing it at least part of the time will help improve or maintain a good body roll.

>> Breathe out underwater constantly. Many swimmers will hold their breath, often until they come up to breathe again. This can cause the body to tense up, which impacts on your balance in the water. Exhaling constantly underwater will ensure you are relaxed, assisting in keeping good technique and improving your balance in the water.

>> Keep your head down when you breathe. Avoid over-rotating your head when you come up to breathe, and breathe in the wave created as you move through the water.

>> Enter the water fingertips first with a horizontal hand. This sets you up for a strong catch underwater.

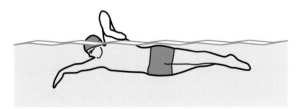

>> When your hand is underwater ensure water is pushed behind you, not down or to the side, ensuring no wasted effort in moving you forward.

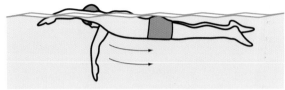

>> Exit your hand with your thumb almost in line with your thigh to ensure the maximum use of the propulsion element of your stroke.

>> Kick from the hip, with relaxed knee and ankles.

Of course, it's much easier *knowing* what you should be doing than actually *doing* it in the water. This is where a swimming coach can prove invaluable, as they are in a position to look at your stroke from above and can feed back any stroke correction needed.

Another more advanced option is to get a stroke analysis through being filmed swimming in an endless pool at a swim specialist centre. This offers your swimming coach the benefit of seeing your underwater action and also allows you to see where you are going wrong. This sort of analysis is becoming more popular and you will be able to find these centres on the internet.

Just to reiterate, the effectiveness and therefore the speed of your swim is centred on your technique (more so than the bike or the run). In the pool, it's very easy to let your mind wander or to watch the bottom of the pool drift by. Don't. Make sure that you are always thinking about your stroke, your body position, the catch, all of it. Really think about what you are doing. It actually fuels the motivation as you can feel yourself 'working' on your stroke and making a positive change.

THE SWIM SESSIONS

Developing an effective balance in your swim training sessions is essential to nailing a long-distance swim. As we've said, if you simply focus on distance then you will get there. It's just that you might get there slowly. However, if you don't put enough distance-work in and purely concentrate on speed work then you might not get there at all.

So what is the right balance? Well, that partly depends on your physical condition and your schedule.

The first thing to be conscious of is your physical condition. Making the step-up to 3.8-km racing is a big ask on your body. It's not uncommon for athletes to develop shoulder injuries as they get used to swimming further and further. The key is not to push it too hard if things don't feel right. After all, it's better to take a voluntary week out of the pool than an enforced month.

Scheduling is likely to dictate your swimming sessions. How much time can you devote to the pool? How long should your sessions be? In an ideal world, you would be swimming at least three or four times a week to see significant improvement in your swim times. Swimming in a Masters swimming group at your local club can be an excellent way to keep your motivation up and push your performance.

The key swim sessions that you need to focus on are:

>> **Interval training:** The majority of your swim training will be based around interval training rather than just getting in the pool and swimming up and down in an unstructured way. Varying intervals and rest between intervals will obviously impact on what you get from each session. A logical progression should be to learn to swim fast and then improve your endurance by increasing interval length.

>> **Endurance sessions:** It goes without saying that these are a pivotal part of your training. You have to build your strength and stamina so that you have the ability and confidence to complete the 3.8-km swim.

>> **Long sessions:** Your long-distance triathlon swim training should include one long session per week, which can consist of a straight off swim or a number of longer intervals that break down your targeted distance.

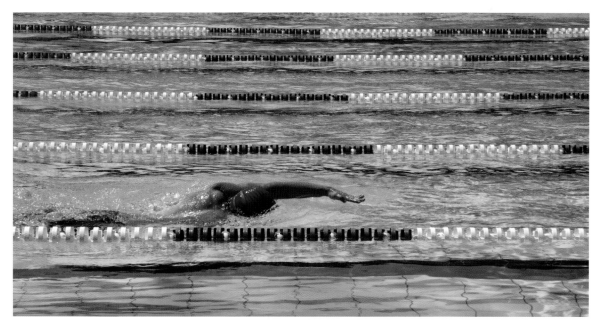

This session will start at the maximum distance that you can swim and build from there. Keep the progression gradual but continuous, and don't start off by having a bash at doing 3.8km (unless you can swim that far already).

>> **Time trials:** Once a month it can be beneficial to do a time trial; completing a set distance as fast as you can. As your training progresses you should be swimming the time trial faster. If you're not it is an indicator that you may need to reassess the training you are doing.

>> **Drills:** Drilling is a good discipline to get into. It is something that you should do almost every time you get into the pool, normally as part of a warm-up. Drills will help you to refine your stroke, correct imbalances in your technique and make you a better, more efficient swimmer. There are numerous different drills that will help you to refine your swim technique. Some of the most popular are:

>> Single arm swimming: Keeping one arm straight out in front of you, concentrate on front crawl using just the other arm breathing every 2–3 strokes. Do a length then swap arms. You may find one arm is a lot stronger than the other, so focus on improving the weaker arm.

>> Hand drags: On your recovery phase, focus on keeping your elbow high and your palm facing backwards as it travels across the water. Let your fingertips drag the surface of the water until your arm is fully extended and enters the water again. This promotes the correct position for your arm allowing it to 'recover' within the stroke and get the correct position for entry into the water again.

>> Catch-ups: Do not pull through on one arm until the other arm has 'caught up', in effect both arms will momentarily be side by side in front of you. This will assist in improving your stroke timing.

>> Kicking practice: Holding a float out in front of you, use just your legs, kicking from the hips not the knees, to propel you. When racing it is important not to overdo the amount of kicking you do and focus on maintaining a relaxed rhythm to avoid tiredness or even cramp when starting to cycle. Developing a strong kick will help keep the legs fresh following the swim.

>> Rotation drills: Hold a float between your legs, sticking up in air. Every time you take a stroke aim to touch the float with your hand rotating it back across your body. This promotes the rotation of your body to improve your body position in the water as discussed earlier.

>> Pull-buoys: These allow you to focus on good upper body technique and building upper body strength. Be aware of the extra stress on your shoulders and stop if this is too much.

>> Paddles: Swim paddles add extra load to the workout, which can improve general conditioning. Be aware of the added stress to the shoulders to avoid injury.

There are many other drills you can try depending on the areas of weakness you may have. A swimming coach can look at your existing technique and recommend the areas to work on and so point out the drills that will be most useful to developing your stroke.

OPEN WATER SWIMMING

Ideally you would already have experience swimming competitively in open water during another triathlon event. If you haven't it would be a sensible idea to try this before your long-distance race, as there are some obvious differences from pool swimming. For a start it is much more physical. Secondly, you need to look where you are swimming (sighting). And finally, there are some real benefits that can be learned from swimming competitively in open water that you need to be aware of.

Physicality

The close proximity of perhaps over 2,000 other swimmers at the mass start of a long-distance race can be a disconcerting experience. Many competitors will have a bad experience and just want to stop as they get swum over, banged or kicked. Being prepared for this will allow you to keep going in the knowledge that eventually you should find clear water, get your breath back and hit your normal front crawl stroke again. Panicking at this point can impact badly on the rest of your day, so staying strong and focused to keep going is a key attribute. Carefully choosing your starting point can make a difference to your experience (for example don't start at the front if you are a slow swimmer!), but be prepared for a tough time!

Sighting

Sighting is an obvious but sometimes overlooked element of the swim. Far too many triathletes simply forget to sight or blindly follow other swimmers, potentially resulting in swimming a much longer distance. The only way to really practise sighting is to find a local lake or go to the sea and learn to swim following buoys or other markers. As open water swimming is growing in popularity in its own right, more and more venues are opening their doors to swimmers.

When you get to an open water venue and have plotted your swim route, that's when you practise your sighting. The technique to sighting is to use the stroke of your stronger arm to propel the top of your head out of the water looking forward to get a good view of where you are aiming for. Before you start, look for easily visible landmarks along the route and use them to navigate in water. Try to avoid stopping and treading water to look around, instead integrate sighting as a natural part of your stroke.

Drafting

Drafting on the bike is not legal in long-distance triathlons, and if you do it you deserve to be penalised or disqualified. Drafting on the swim, however, is a completely different matter. Swim drafting works in exactly the same way as cycle drafting: the person ahead of you is forcing their way through the water. The water directly behind them is moving in the

direction they are swimming. Therefore, if you get into that water, you will be pulled along.

But be warned: nobody likes it when someone is continually tapping them on the toes. Sure, you want to stay close. And sure, in a long-distance triathlon people are used to being tapped and bashed. But if you tap someone's toes continuously for 3.8km there's a good chance you'll get a foot in the face.

Instead, try and find someone who swims a little bit faster than you. Even better, try and find a group. Go down to the lake (you can even practise drafting in a pool but it isn't so easy) and practise swimming in a group, drafting off one another. You'll be amazed at how much faster you swim for less effort if you follow closely in the wake of somebody who is a little bit quicker than you. And if that holds true for practice, it certainly holds true in the race.

TRAINING AND RACING IN A WETSUIT

Training and becoming comfortable swimming in a wetsuit is essential. Most long-distance triathlon swims are wetsuit-compulsory. When the water temperature goes above 24^0C the race director may make wetsuits optional or even ban their use, so if you are planning on competing in warmer climates be prepared to deal with this eventuality.

The good news is that swimming in a wetsuit has its advantages. The most important of these is that you are more buoyant in the water, and so you should technically swim faster. However, swimming in a wetsuit can make tiny alterations to your stroke, which can aggravate injuries or strain the shoulders. That is why you need to practise swimming in one. As race day approaches, you should be swimming in your wetsuit more than you are out of it. Get used to it, learn to appreciate it, and practise getting out of it quickly.

You can swim in wetsuits in most pools. However, it's just as easy to kill two birds with one stone and do a wetsuit swim in open water. That way, you can practise sighting, wetsuit swimming and getting out of your suit all in one go!

CHAPTER 008:
CYCLE TRAINING_

'This is my body, and I can do whatever I want to it. I can push it. Study it. Tweak it. Listen to it. Everybody wants to know what I'm on. What am I on? I'm on my bike busting my ass six hours a day. What are you on?'

– Lance Armstrong, Cyclist

THE BIKE LEG of a long-distance triathlon is tough. In fact, it's probably tougher than you think it's going to be. Whichever way you look at it, 180km is a very long way to cycle. Factor in the additional mental and physical stress involved in a long-distance triathlon and you start to get a glimpse into what you are proposing to undertake.

A long-distance triathlon bike leg is defined by the balance between the speed of your bike ride and how much energy you have left for the marathon. Doing a super fast bike leg but coming off exhausted and blowing up after ten miles of running is not a good bike leg. A good bike leg is achieved by controlling your effort level, keeping fuelled and coming out of transition with enough in the tank to complete a marathon.

But how do you get to a stage where you know how much you can – and should – put into the bike without destroying the run? In this chapter, we're going to look at what you need to do to develop an understanding of what you are capable of on the bike, how hard you should go, and what you can do to maximise your chances of posting a fast bike split.

WHAT IS A FAST BIKE SPILT?

If you're a pro (or one of the top age group athletes), a fast bike split on a fairly fast course is somewhere in the region of 4:15 to 4:45. To give you an idea, that's averaging over 40kph. Obviously, we'd all like to be able to sit at 40kph and then go for a run afterwards, but the simple fact is that most of us physically cannot do it (or at least don't have sufficient training time to get to that level). However, you don't have to be doing that kind of speed to be in the mix for a good bike time. As this table of bike splits from the four long-distance triathlons demonstrates, there is a huge range of bike times throughout the field.

Table 8.1 shows the bike splits ranked by bike-only places. for example, the top ten quickest on the bike rode under 4.35 in Ironman Austria, and the top 2,000 rode under 6.04 in Challenge Roth in 2010.

But what can you take away from this? First, that not everyone is posting sub-five-hour bike splits at a long-distance triathlon. In fact, very few people are. There was almost four hours' difference between the fastest and the slowest bike splits at Ironman Austria in 2010. That should show you that there is room for everyone who puts in the right amount of training to be able to complete this leg of a long-distance triathlon.

Second, the comparison between the bike splits at different races demonstrates how important a quick check of the course profile is. One of the UK's top long-distance triathletes, Stephen Bayliss, competed in both

Table 8.1: Bike Splits by Race in 2010

BIKE	IRONMAN AUSTRIA	QUELLE ROTH	IRONMAN UK	NORSEMAN
Hrs/Mins				
<10	4.35	4.29	5.26	6.06
<100	4.53	4.58	6.03	7.24
<500	5.13	5.15	6.57	–
<1,000	5.34	5.29	8.12	–
<1,500	6.01	5.44	–	–
<2,000	6.47	6.04	–	–
Last Place	8.25	8.21	9.20	9.38

Ironman Austria and Ironman UK in 2010. In Austria he did a 4.35 bike split, and in the UK he did a 5.09. Obviously, we can't say that he was in exactly the same shape or that the conditions were identical, but that is a large time difference (for a pro) and is indicative of the degree of difficulty of the course. Table 8.1 also shows that the Norseman is a notoriously tough race and, although it has a much smaller field, times are significantly slower than Austria or Challenge Roth.

TAILORING YOUR TRAINING TO THE BIKE COURSE

There is a huge difference between racing a course that allows you to stay on your tri-bars for the duration of the cycle (like Challenge Roth), or one that will have you sitting up on your hoods as you tackle the hills (like Ironman Lanzarote, with 2,551 metres of climbing). For each race, a certain skill-set is required, and you may even need to look at the set-up of your bike to ensure you have the correct range of gears.

Ideally, you want to train on routes that best replicate the course on which you are racing. In reality though, this is often not possible. If you live in a particularly hilly area, flat time-trialling is difficult (and vice versa). If you have the option, you can cycle (or drive/catch the train) somewhere where you can do a couple of rides that will replicate the kind of course that you are going to be racing on. You can even make a little holiday out of it (but that's when you know you are in deep!).

Regardless of the course, you still need to get the base miles in so you know your legs have enough to get you through the 180km and still be in shape to complete the marathon.

WHAT ARE YOUR TRAINING GOALS?

Fast bike riders produce a high level of power throughout the bike course while maintaining an aerodynamic position. With that as the ultimate goal of your bike training, the key is to focus on developing both your power, and your ability to sustain that level of power over the course of the bike leg.

Power is developed by interval training, hill reps, big gear repetitions and strength training. Endurance or increasing your sustained power output is honed through mixing up longer rides, tempo riding and longer interval training.

At the same time, you should be focusing on becoming more aerodynamic (as discussed in Chapter 3). The ability to hold an aerodynamic position for a sustained period of time both enhances your cycling efficiency, and will lead to a quicker bike time.

TRAINING SESSIONS

The major consideration for any long-distance triathlete is to be able to ride 180km and be in a position to run (or walk if you have to) a marathon following it. If your bike endurance is not currently at a level where you can ride anywhere near this sort of distance, then this should be your main training goal. If your limiter is not your endurance but perhaps the speed in which you can ride this distance then including some higher intensity training and strength work can help.

It is important to remember that you will not ride at your maximum pace for the full 180km. Instead, you are likely to maintain a slower pace that enables you to run off the bike.

Getting to the point where you can ride the distance and then increase the race pace you can handle (and then run that marathon), involves a lot of training that by-and-large is focused on three key sessions in your training week: the long ride, the interval session or hill repetitions, and the tempo ride. In addition, some bike drills and big gear work will contribute to your pedalling efficiency and strength.

The Long Ride

This is the bedrock of your training plan. If this is your first long-distance triathlon and you don't have the bike volume, there's a good chance that you'll finish some of these rides feeling extremely tired. Building the required endurance and strength can take a long time if you are not used to long rides already, so it's important to give yourself the proper training time to develop this strength. Ideally you will do one long ride a week, riding at an easy pace and building the distance week-by-week. You should look to ride a route that incorporates some hills to develop your general strength and fitness more quickly.

But how far is long? The eventual goal should be to get the long ride up to at least 100 miles, and gradually add in some higher intensity efforts when you find it comfortable to ride this distance at an easy pace. The long ride can become boring if you only ever do it on your own, and you may well find that riding with others can make the process more enjoyable. However, as you near race-day it is important to do a few longer rides alone. Riding solo for a long time can be a mentally challenging process at times, and it's important you don't experience that for the first time in a race situation.

Interval Sessions

The long ride will build your endurance, but interval training sessions will build your power and power endurance. Try to fit in at least one session a week, either on a turbo trainer (see page 58) or on a quiet stretch of road. Using a heart rate monitor or power meter will maintain the quality of the sessions and allow you to record progress throughout your training plan.

Specific sessions are outlined later in the training plan, but aim to start off with shorter intervals, for example

3 × 10 minutes at zone three with 2 minutes easy spin recovery at lower, zone two intensity. Gradually build this distance to complete for example 4 × 15 minutes with two minutes recovery at the same intensities. As your fitness improves you should be able to ride at a faster pace for the same effort, or maintain the same pace for a longer time. Interval training gives great feedback on how your training is progressing.

Tempo Riding

Tempo riding is slightly faster than race pace, allowing you to build power endurance and develop an understanding of what pace you can sustain over a longer period. The goal is to gradually build the length of this ride up to 2–3 hours at a zone three level of intensity.

Establishing what heart rate or perceived effort level you can comfortably sustain during this longer period

is a key factor in determining your racing effort level – and speed. With that in mind, it is worthwhile taking the time to focus on getting your pacing right.

One point to note is that often you can ride a lot faster in a race, with the benefit of aid stations and a traffic-free course, so using speed as an indicator of a sustainable pace might be misleading (it also doesn't take into account weather conditions or the course profile). Heart rate or power output are often the best ways to control your pace, e.g. controlling the effort you are putting in, rather than judging the output in the form of speed.

Hill Repetitions

Hill repetitions are great for building bike strength and power. Find a hill of around 200m with a consistent gradient and sprint up with a recovery freewheel down – aim to do 5–10 repetitions, depending on your fitness. This session will be particularly relevant if you plan to race on a hilly course, but even if you aren't, it is an important session for the base and early build period of training.

The Time Trial

The time trial is a flat-out, timed session to monitor your improvement over the course of the training period, using a set course for comparison. This is not strictly necessary, but doing one now and then can give you some decent feedback on how you are progressing. Be aware that it can take time to recover from this exertion, so don't do it on a regular basis and it shouldn't be longer than a 1–2 hour ride.

Brick Session

The brick session for the bike-to-run transition is discussed in more detail in Chapter 9 but there are two important points to note for the purposes of this section. First, after swimming 3.8km your lower back, shoulders and legs can stiffen up and create some discomfort on the bike, so it is worthwhile doing some long swim/bike bricks to see how you react to swimming such a long way first. The second is working

out the best way to prepare you for the run while still on the bike. Having a strategy for the final minutes on the bike can offer some benefit when you start running, notably:

1. Think about controlling your pace over the last ten minutes of the ride so you come off the bike a bit more relaxed.

2. If it works for you, try some stretching while cycling, particularly of the back and hamstrings/calves.

3. Take some last-minute nutrition and top up your liquids so you start running with some energy and are properly hydrated.

This can all be planned and practised in training. Having a checklist of things to do in your mind during the race can help you start the run on the right foot so to speak!

The Turbo Trainer

Training on the turbo can be mentally challenging, but it is often the only option available during the winter months. But even when the weather is fine the turbo trainer is an option for a quick session if you only have an hour or so available, giving the option of completing a quick interval or hard tempo session which could be interrupted when cycling outside by traffic or too many red lights.

When on the trainer always start with ten minutes easy spinning to warm your legs up (and the same or longer to warm-down) and then incorporate sessions as discussed above for intervals or tempo riding. Be aware that unless you have excellent air conditioning you are likely to sweat a lot and so using a floor covering (and wiping the sweat from your bike) is recommended!

Cycling Drills

Although not having such an impact as improving your running or swimming technique, having a good pedalling technique is well worth focusing on. View your legs as drawing circles rather than pumping up and down as pistons, and keep a smooth, consistent speed through the rotation. This should help eliminate the potential dead spots at the top and bottom of the pedal stroke. The two exercises below will help in achieving this:

>> **Spinning:** Ride with a high cadence (over 120 revolutions per minute) in an easy gear for 45 seconds, repeat for five reps. It might feel strange at first and your behind might bounce out of the saddle, but as you focus on a circular pedal stroke you will eventually be able to pedal a high cadence while staying in the saddle.

>> **One-legged drills:** Remove one foot from the pedals, making sure it's out of the way of the crank. Turn over the pedals with only one leg, ensuring consistent speed through the rotation. After 30 seconds swap legs and repeat. This exercise primarily ensures each leg has a comparably good technique.

Increasing Your Bike Strength

>> **Big gear workouts:** This exercise can be done on the flat or on a hill. Shift into a hard gear and pedal staying seated. Try 8 × 60 seconds with 30 seconds of easy pedalling as recovery. This exercise is good for increasing your leg strength and so your power on the bike. You should see an increase in the gear you can turn as you do more sessions.

HOW MUCH CYCLE TRAINING DO YOU NEED TO DO?

There is no simple answer to this question, and there are numerous variables that will influence it (such as existing fitness levels, goals, time available to train etc.). Cycle training for a long-distance triathlon is a time-consuming activity. Fitting in one long ride a week should be a minimum aim, if possible two further rides, including an interval/hill session and a tempo ride.

As the cycle leg is the longest section of the race by time taken and sits before the marathon, it makes sense to focus a large proportion of your training on the bike. Your bike fitness should also translate to some extent in improving your run fitness (which isn't so evident the other way round). As well as this you want to finish the bike leg with some strength left in you for the run. However good a runner you are, if you can't complete the 180km comfortably or cycle it too hard you won't be running a decent marathon leg. Set your bike training up to give yourself the best opportunity to get around the marathon.

>> CHAPTER 009:
RUN TRAINING_

'I don't think I get off the bike and think "I can win this", I always think the same: "what do I need to do to maximise my performance?" I can only control my pace and my hydration.'

– Craig Alexander, Two-Time Ironman World Champion

RUNNING A MARATHON on its own is tough. Running a marathon after a 2.4-mile swim and 112 miles of cycling? Well, that's another level.

The prospect of running the marathon in a long-distance triathlon – particularly in your first race – can be quite overwhelming. It is impossible to know what time you will run (even if you are a seasoned marathon runner or middle-distance triathlete) because you are simply not used to running that distance on already fatigued legs.

However, with the right preparation, the marathon can become a manageable – if not enjoyable – leg of the long-distance triathlon. But the key really is in the preparation. You cannot expect to enter a race and just hope that the run leg comes together (needless to say, the same is true for the swim and the bike). If you do, the chances are you will not finish the race. Even if you plan on walking the marathon, you need to have your body in a place that will allow you to spend anything up to 17 hours engaged in constant physical activity.

For the purposes of this chapter, we are going to assume that your goal is to cross the finishing line knowing that you have given everything that you have got. You have conquered whatever the course has thrown at you, dealt with the best that mother nature has in her armoury, and achieved your goals. However, to get to that stage, you have to have put in the base miles. You have to train smart as well as hard. And ideally you have to stay injury-free.

There are months of training and miles of running involved in completing the marathon leg, and all of that starts here.

WHAT IS YOUR CURRENT LEVEL OF RUN FITNESS?

Have you recently (in the last year or so) run a marathon? Is the longest run you've ever completed ten miles? Have you ever done a middle-distance triathlon with a half-marathon distance run leg? Of course, if you have extensive experience of running long-distance races, you will be in a stronger position when you start training for a long-distance triathlon.

However, this isn't to say that if you haven't run any further than ten miles you can't prepare yourself to tackle the marathon for the first time in a long-distance race, it just means you need to ensure you have the required training time to develop a running endurance base.

As a basic rule (and this is with the caveat that you have paced the bike leg well), novice long-distance triathletes can expect to run the marathon leg some 45–80 minutes slower than their straight-out marathon time if they do sufficient training. Faster, more experienced runners often find that their marathon time is around 15–30 minutes slower than their marathon personal best.

The training plan in this book assumes you can go out and run ten miles now. This does not necessarily mean that you can run it at a quick pace, just that you can do the distance. This sets a strong starting point to build from over the next 24 weeks. If you can't yet run ten miles then it might be advisable to spend a month or two building up to this level of fitness before starting the training plan.

WHAT CONSTITUTES A GOOD LONG-DISTANCE TRIATHLON MARATHON TIME?

The short answer to this is whatever it takes to achieve your race goal. But if this is your first long-distance triathlon, be realistic with your goals. There is nothing more disheartening than watching your time slip-by in a race – and it can be utterly disastrous when you are physically and mentally exhausted.

But, as an example, let's take a look at the marathon times for those four long-distance triathlons (overleaf):

Table 9.1: Run Times By Ranking in 2010

RUN	IRONMAN AUSTRIA	QUELLE ROTH	IRONMAN UK	NORSEMAN
Hrs/Mins				
<10	2.55	2.55	3.01	4.35
<100	3.22	3.17	3.34	5.47
<500	3.55	3.41	4.22	–
<1,000	4.22	4.01	5.49	–
<1,500	4.54	4.20	–	–
<2,000	6.23	4.45	–	–
Last Place	7.32	7.01	7.11	8.10

What can we learn from these times? Well, first that the top finishers (mostly professionals) put in lightning quick marathon times. Sub three-hour marathon running in a long-distance race is very impressive and if you get anywhere near this then you can count yourself as one of the top long-distance triathlon runners. But again, the really interesting variable here is the range of times that people do. Whether you're a three-hour or a seven-hour runner, the simple fact is that with the right amount of work you can complete the race. But you do have to put in the miles...

TRAINING SESSIONS

Preparing for the marathon in a long-distance triathlon presents several challenges over and above training for a straight-off marathon. There will be less time available in the week to train, you will be running the actual race on tired legs, and you will probably start with a deficit in nutrition and hydration. As already discussed this will have a significant impact on the pace at which you can run.

With that in mind, your goal is not necessarily to run flat out but instead to develop the ability to maintain a steady pace when you are tired and struggling for lack of nutrition and hydration. Your run training will focus on building a good aerobic base of running fitness, allowing your body to develop the muscles that are engaged at a slower pace and improve the efficiency of your body in turning fat and carbohydrates into energy.

Developing your aerobic base consists of lots of steady running with the focus on building the length of runs while maintaining a low level of intensity at a low zone two. Try to run (or build up to run) three times a week if possible, consisting of a long run, which will form the backbone of your running schedule, and two middle-distance runs of 45–90 minutes in length.

The length of the long run should gradually build up to a maximum of 2.5 hours. Beyond this distance there is a quickly diminishing return on fitness and a much higher chance of injury. All of these runs should feel easy (you should be able to hold a conversation as you are running) maintaining a pace at the bottom of zone two or in zone one.

After 15 weeks of building your aerobic base, or when you can comfortably complete a long run of 2.5 hours, look to increase the pace of one of the mid-distance runs to the top of zone two or slightly faster than your marathon pace (if you know it). Also, aim to include some similar higher-intensity efforts into your long run, for example 6 x 15 minutes, to develop your pace over the distance.

Running at a higher intensity than this is not necessary to achieve what in fact will be a 'slow' marathon (taken on a stand-alone basis). Higher intensity training may also compromise your other sessions in the week as you will be tired and will take longer to recover. Your goal should be to get consistency in your run training, maintaining the number of sessions on a weekly basis.

The Brick Run

Another run you should aim to complete several times at the middle and end of your training is the brick run. A key session for every long-distance triathlete, the brick is a spell of running after a bike ride, helping to

get your legs used to the feeling of running when fatigued from cycling.

Start by doing 15 minutes of easy jogging and then gradually build this up to a maximum of 45 minutes. This is sufficient to get your body used to the transition from cycling to running. Going further will not add much training value and will increase the risk of injury.

RUNNING TECHNIQUE AND DRILLS

Many runners are limited by poor technique and most runners can improve some aspect of it. Maintaining good technique when your body is tired will give you the potential to clock a fast time and can also help you reduce the risk of injury.

Running Technique

Here are six of the key fundamentals of good running technique:

1. Landing on the balls of your feet when your foot hits the ground increases forward momentum and avoids the heavy landing of the flat-footed runner.

2. Keeping your head upwards with your eyes focusing 15 metres in front of you reduces hunching of your shoulders and neck.

3. Arms should swing in a relaxed, effortless rhythmic motion, aiding your forward momentum rather than hindering it. Ensuring your arms are providing this benefit can help particularly up hills and when tired.

4. Keeping your shoulders relaxed opens up the chest and makes breathing easier.

5. Your running stride should feel natural and smooth. When you speed up it is easy to start over striding, which increases the impact on joints.

6. Keeping relaxed allows you to control your breathing and maintain a consistent and efficient technique.

Running Drills

Running speed equals stride length multiplied by stride frequency. Increasing either or preferably both will improve your running speed. Technique drills will isolate aspects of your running stride and allow you to work on developing them specifically.

Warm-up first and then try completing 3 × 20 seconds of each of the drills below twice a week:

>> **High knees running/quick feet drill:** The aim of this drill is to increase leg turnover and improve your knee lift. Maintain an upright body position and bring your knees up directly in front of you. Aim to maximise the number of steps you take rather than stride length, keep your leg turnover fast.

>> **Bum kicks:** Again, these are designed to increase leg turnover, but the focus this time is on the hamstrings and the recovery stage of the stride. Keep the top of the legs still and look to bring the heel of the foot up to touch your backside, again keep the tempo high.

>> **Forward flicks:** This drill accentuates the forward reach of your stride, to increase your stride length. Keep in an upright position and flick your front foot straight out landing on the balls of your foot. As you land, flick the other foot out in front and repeat with a fairly fast turnover.

>> **Strides:** Run a number of 50m efforts, aiming to stride out rather than sprint. Focus on the full range of movement in your running stride, landing on the balls of your feet and pushing off strongly.

>> **Arm drills:** Accentuate your arm movement, aiming to drive yourself forward rather than swinging them side-to-side. Incorporate this as part of your strides drill.

TIPS ON LONG-DISTANCE TRIATHLON RUNNING TRAINING

The following points should be considered when undertaking your training:

>> The right trainers: As outlined in Chapter 3, having the right pair of trainers will assist in avoiding injury and support your running stride.

>> A consistent approach to training is important, rather than lots of mileage one week and a dip the next.

>> Hand in hand with this consistent approach is keeping the intensity of your running low when building your aerobic base.

>> Listen to your body: If a run becomes a struggle and you can't complete a session or it's a lot slower than it should be, consider taking some time off to recover.

>> Use the right equipment: Keeping fuelled on the long runs can be aided by a belt to carry a water bottle or having pockets for gels. It can also be advisable to take money on the long runs (in case you bonk or need extra fluids).

>> If you have a niggle don't just try and push through the pain, it will only make it worse. Rest from running if you have to and spend the time focusing on your swimming and cycling fitness.

>> Keep motivated: The long run in particular (for some people) can be quite a boring training session. Running with others or finding interesting routes can be of great help. Take time on a long run to envisage the race ahead and go through some positive mental visualisation of how race day will feel and what you want to achieve.

CHAPTER 010:
STRENGTH TRAINING AND
CONDITIONING_

'The only place where success comes before work is in the dictionary.'

– Vidal Sassoon, Hairdresser and Businessman

STRENGTH TRAINING AWAY from the pool, the bike or the run is something often overlooked by long-distance triathletes. However, this is an area that – if you can fit it into an already demanding training schedule – can translate directly into increased speed. But if adding strength training to your training plan proves to be too much, it is not the end of the world. Rest assured that concentrating on running, cycling and swimming is more important.

It is, of course, possible to do some strength work as part of your training. Using swim paddles, riding in a big gear, or practising hill reps on the run all count for bona fide strength sessions and should be viewed as such. If you do have the space to fit in some strength work, here is a guide to the benefits it can offer and how best to approach it.

BENEFITS OF STRENGTH TRAINING

To understand the benefits of strength training, it can be useful to split out discipline-specific exercises and core strength exercises. Discipline-specific strength training is focused on increasing power and power endurance in those muscles that are used directly in swimming, cycling or running. This includes specific leg-strength exercises (such as squats or leg presses) or upper body exercises (such as lat pull-downs or running arms).

The core refers to muscles deep in your back and abs, those attached to the spine or pelvis. Core strength is important, as this area is your body's centre of power, where movement originates and therefore the source of your stability. Exercises such as sit ups, hip raises and bicycle kicks can all help strengthen the core.

How These Exercises Can Benefit The Swim, Bike and Run

>> **Swim:** Having a strong core helps ensure your body is kept in a streamlined position for the duration of the event, with any movement being directed to forward propulsion rather than rocking from side to side. Increased strength will also benefit stroke/leg power and endurance.

>> **Bike:** With better body stability from a strong core, your pedalling efficiency will be maintained for longer when you start getting tired. A weak core can mean more pressure is put through the lower back, which can become sore and uncomfortable when riding. Improving your bike strength will increase the amount of power you apply to the pedals and, coupled with endurance, the length of time you can apply the increased power level.

>> **Run:** A strong core will allow you to maintain a good running technique, keeping your back tall and straight, allowing a long stride length and efficiency in forward momentum.

A strength programme does offer many benefits, particularly for someone who has a weak core and

loses form quickly as tiredness sets in. Increasing strength will involve putting in place a range of exercises and a steady progression in the number of repetitions and amount of weight completed.

Setting Up a Strength Training Plan

A strength training plan should look to develop strength early on in the 24-week programme and then aim to maintain that strength towards the middle and end of the period. With this progression in mind, a strength plan could be phased as follows:

Preparation – five weeks

This phase looks to develop a base strength and correct technique for the exercises. The number of repetitions starts low and gradually increases, while the weight is

also kept low. Aim to do two sessions per week, with two sets of 20 repetitions (with 30 seconds' rest) with a light weight for weight-bearing exercises and two sets of 10–20 repetitions (also with 30 seconds rest) for non-weight-bearing exercises.

Strength – ten weeks

This is the period to build your strength, increasing the weight while reducing repetitions for any weight lifting, and increasing the number of repetitions for non-weight-bearing exercises.

Continue with two sessions a week, building up to three sessions. For weight-bearing exercises, build to three sets of 8–10 repetitions (with one minute's recovery) using the heaviest weight you can while completing the sets. For non-weight-bearing exercises, complete three sets of 30 repetitions with 30 seconds recovery.

Maintenance – nine weeks

The goal in this period is to maintain the strength you have developed in the preceding weeks. Aim to do two sessions a week, decreasing the number of sets from the strength period. For weight-bearing exercises, complete one to two sets of ten repetitions with 45 seconds' rest between sets. For non-weight-bearing exercises, complete two sets of 30 repetitions with 30 seconds's of rest.

EXERCISES

A selection of weight resistance and core exercises are listed below; focus on the exercises to improve your weaknesses and select a maximum of eight exercises to do in one session.

Weight Resistance Exercises

>> **Squats:** Develop the muscles of the thighs, hips and buttocks and are of particular benefit in improving your cycling strength.

>> **Leg extensions:** Work on the quadriceps and again are good for cycling strength.

>> **Lat pull-downs (in front of head) or pull-ups:** Particularly benefit the pull phase of your front crawl stroke.

>> **Seated rows:** Improves your upper body strength and the arm movements mimic the catch phase of the swim.

>> **Tricep extensions:** The triceps are active during swimming, aiding in extending your arm out in front of you when you begin a stroke and pulling your arm underneath you in the pull phase.

>> **Hamstring curls:** Stronger hamstrings will improve your running stride and strength.

>> **Calf raises:** Strong calf muscles will benefit both your running and your cycling.

>> **Flat bench/hanging leg raises (without weights):** Using the weight of your body as the resistance, leg raises will work your hip flexors and abdominals, providing benefits for all three disciplines.

>> **Deadlift:** Works your abductors, hamstrings, quadriceps and back muscles. Great for overall strength improvements.

CORE EXERCISES

Push-ups

Great for the chest, shoulders, triceps and abs. Place your hands on the floor, shoulder-width apart with the balls of your feet on the ground. Raise yourself with your arms into the plank position, keeping a straight line from your head to you heels – this is the start/finish point of the push-up. Lower your torso to the ground and then push up using your shoulders and chest until you arms are almost straight (but not locked). Finish in the plank position.

Hip raises

Great for the front abs. Lie on your back with your arms extended, palms down next to your hips. Lift the head and shoulders 1–2 inches off the floor. Extend your legs forward and just off the ground with your feet pointing to the ceiling. Bring your legs up and lift your hips a few inches off the ground, hold for a few seconds and then bring the legs down to the original starting position, straight in front just off the ground. Make sure your back is kept flat on the floor at all times, with the control and movement maintained in the abs.

Oblique crunches

Lie on your side with your legs one on top of the other and both bent at the knees. Hold one hand behind your head and the other resting on your side. Raise your upper torso and head with the power coming from your side muscles. Try not to fold forward, but bend up, trying to get your elbow to touch your feet.

Side dips

Lie on your right side with your right forearm on the floor, facing away from your body. Place the other hand on your hip. Keep your body straight, touching the floor on your forearm and the side of your right foot. Moving just the hips, lower to just touch the ground and then raise again into the straight position. Repeat on the other side.

Standard crunch bicycle

Lie on your back with your legs just off the ground in front of you and your shoulder blades off the ground. Rest your hands behind your head to help stability, but don't put any pressure on your neck. Keep one leg straight and bring the knee back on the other leg until it goes past the hips, repeat in a pedalling motion. Movement control should be through the abs but you might feel pressure on your hamstrings as well.

Leg raises

Lie in the plank position with the balls of your feet and forearms in contact with the ground. Ensure you body is straight from head to heel. Raise one leg at a time as high as you can and lower for one repetition. Repeat for the other leg.

Half-up twists

Sit in the half-up position where you can feel your core muscles engaged. Fold your arms and twist to the side, using your core for stability and control. Repeat on the other side for one repetition.

Heel taps

Lie on your back with your legs bent and your feet flat on the floor. Keeping your shoulder blades off the ground, reach to touch the heel of your foot on one side and then again on the other with the other hand. Keep your heels far enough away that you really have to stretch to touch them.

CHAPTER 011:
THE 24-WEEK TRAINING PLAN_

'Some people want it to happen, some wish it would happen, others make it happen.'

– Michael Jordan, US Basketball Player

THE **PURPOSE OF** this book is to equip you with the tools and knowledge to help you develop and manage your training plan so that you are prepared for race day. There is no 'one size fits all' approach to this plan as we all have different strengths and weaknesses, levels of fitness, time available to train and goals for race day.

With that in mind, this plan should be used as a base from which you can grow and develop a training strategy that suits your own individual needs. However, while we might all be different, there are a few core points that apply to everyone:

1. Gradually increase the volume and intensity of your training;

2. Include periods of rest;

3. Train consistently rather than going through extreme peaks and troughs;

4. Target key sessions to complete each week if you are pressured for time;

5. Focus on quality of training rather than just quantity.

As described earlier, this six-month training plan is split into four phases, the base phase (lasting ten weeks), the build phase (lasting a further ten weeks), the peak phase (lasting three weeks) and finally race week (lasting one week).

BASE PHASE – TEN WEEKS

This table outlines some possible sessions in the base phase period.

>> **Swim:** Improving your swimming technique should be the major focus in this period, which could mean finding a coach or getting a swim analysis completed. For two swims in the week, start and finish the session with swimming drills. Work on improving your general swim speed using some short to medium intervals, gradually building the length of sessions.

>> **Bike:** In this period aim to get your bike position 'right'. There should be two main goals for your training: first, start to improve your bike endurance by building up the long ride; and second, to work on improving your power output through intervals, hill reps and big gear work.

>> **Run:** The run focus is to build endurance at a low intensity. Aim for three runs a week at an easy pace, gradually increasing the length of these runs, particularly the long run. Incorporate some drills into your training with a view to improving your technique if needed.

>> **Strength training:** If you are going to incorporate a strength programme as part of your training, follow the advice in Chapter 10 for this period.

Table 11.1 Example Base Phase Sessions

🏊 SWIM SESSIONS	🚴 BIKE SESSIONS	🏃 RUN SESSIONS
200m warm-up/5 × 100m with 30secs rest/5 × 50m with 15secs rest/350m drills/200m warm-down = Total 1,500m	Medium ride – 90–120mins	Medium run – 30–60mins run on a hilly course
1200m steady/300m drills = Total 1,500m	Long ride – 120–240mins	Long run – 60–120mins
200m warm-up/4 × 300m with 45secs rest/600m warm-down/ Drills = Total 2,000m	90mins bike ride with 5 × 3mins Zone 3 efforts	
500m warm-up/5 × 100m with paddles/pull-buoy/5 × 50m kicking/400m drills/500m warm-down = Total 2,150m	90mins steady bike ride with 5 × 200m hill reps	
400m warm-up/drills/10 × 100m with 20secs recovery/3 × 200m with 30secs recovery/500m warm-down = Total 2,500m	60min bike drills (high cadence, big gear work, one leg riding)	

Table 11.2 Sample Week

MON	TUES	WED	THURS	FRI	SAT	SUN
Swim –Strength (1.5km)	Run – Endurance (90–120mins)	Bike – Intervals (60–90mins)	Swim – Endurance (2–2.5km)	Run – Steady (60mins)	Rest	Bike – Endurance (3–4 hrs)
Strength			Strength			

Set out above is a possible training week in the period. The run endurance session is timetabled as a mid-week session, to give at least one day at the weekend free for other commitments.

BUILD PHASE – 10 WEEKS

>> **Swim:** Technique work is still important during this phase, but the emphasis moves on to increasing the length of sessions to build the speed endurance. Some open water swims should also be completed to get used to swimming outdoors, using a wetsuit and sighting.

>> **Bike:** If your bike endurance is good, then it is time to start introducing some faster paced efforts on your long ride. If you are still struggling to complete the long ride, keep focusing on building this endurance base. A mix of intervals, hill reps and tempo riding should make up the other session.

>> **Run:** Brick runs are introduced to get the body used to running off the bike. The long run is increased to keep building the endurance base. If you are coping with the long run comfortably, slightly increase the pace of the second run and build it from 60 to 90mins.

Table 11.3 Example Build Phase Sessions

This table outlines some possible sessions in the build phase period.

🌊 SWIM SESSIONS	🚴 BIKE SESSIONS	🏃 RUN SESSIONS
400m warm-up/10 × 200m with 30secs rest/600m warm-down, inc drills = Total 3,000m	Interval sessions: For example 120mins steady cycle incorporating 5 × 10-min intervals at level 3 intensity	Long run: Keeping the pace easy, build up to 2.5 hours
200m warm-up/5 × 300m with 40secs rest/5 × 200m with 30secs rest/800m warm-down, inc drills = Total 3,500m	Race pace/Tempo ride: Build from a shorter distance at race pace and gradually increase over the weeks (from 60mins to 150mins)	Tempo run: 60–90mins of stand-alone marathon pace running
1,000m warm-up, inc drills/4 × 500m with 1min recovery/500m warm-down = Total 3,500m	Hill reps: 90mins steady cycle incorporating 8 × 3min hill reps	Brick session: Following a tempo ride or long bike ride, include a 15-min run, gradually building up to a maximum of 45mins
500m warm-up/600m with 45secs rest/500m with 40secs rest/400m with 35secs rest/300m with 30secs rest/200m with 25secs rest/100m/400m warm-down, inc drills = Total 3,000m	Long ride: Building up gradually to 5–6 hrs, also start including some race pace efforts within the ride	
200m warm-up/ 9 × 400m with 40secs rest/200m warm-down = Total 4,000m		

Table 11.4 Sample Week

The sample week for the build phase reflects the increase in distances in the period. The key sessions to target are the long endurance sessions for all three disciplines. If you need to omit sessions, take out the steady runs and steady swims, maintaining the bike intervals if possible on top of the endurance sessions.

MON	TUES	WED	THURS	FRI	SAT	SUN
Swim – Strength (2–2.5km)	Run – Endurance (120–150mins)	Bike – Intervals (90–120mins)	Run – Tempo (75mins)	Swim – Endurance (3.5–4km) Bike – Tempo (90–120mins)	Swim – Steady (2.5–3km) Run – Steady (60 mins)	Bike – Endurance (5–6 hrs) Run – Brick (15mins)
Strength				Strength		

PEAK PHASE – THREE WEEKS

>> **Swim:** The length of intervals are reduced to focus instead on speed. Keep doing the open water swims in preparation for race day.

>> **Bike:** Volume is reduced with a focus on higher intensity and faster sessions. You should have the endurance base in place and now is the time to sharpen up and develop the feeling of speed and power on the bike.

>> **Run:** Your last long run should be three weeks before race day, giving you plenty of time to recover. Other runs in this period should be shorter and faster, with the goal to start feeling fresh and ready to race.

Table 11.5 Example Peak Phase Sessions

This table outlines some possible sessions in the peak phase period.

🌊 SWIM SESSIONS	🚴 BIKE SESSIONS	🏃 RUN SESSIONS
500 warm-up/10 × 200m with 30secs rest/500m warm-down = Total 3,000m	Flat out 90mins	60-min Run–Tempo
500m warm-up/500m drills/10 × 50m with 15secs rest/5 × 100m with 25secs rest/500m warm-down = Total 2,500m	No more than 180mins long ride	60mins steady
500m warm-up/10 × 100m steady/500m warm-down = Total 2,000m	60mins ride including 10 × 1min hard ride	No more than 100mins long run

Table 11.6 Sample Week

MON	TUES	WED	THURS	FRI	SAT	SUN
Swim – Fast (1.5–2km)	Run – Tempo (75mins)	Bike – Intervals (60–90mins)	Run – Steady (60mins)	Swim –Steady (2.5-3km)	Rest	Bike – Tempo (120–180mins)

THE TRAINING PLAN

With the above detail and weekly structures in mind the following plan is a guide to the sessions you should complete, but isn't a rigid day-by-day programme. You have to be the boss of this schedule, determining which sessions to do and when.

The plan rolls from week to week, with intensity levels stated in brackets beside each session. For example, week three has two bike sessions, one at intensity level two and one harder session with some level three efforts. Total weekly distance swum or minutes cycled/run are indicated, these should act as a guide rather than being prescriptive.

Table 11.7 Base Phase Training Schedule

WEEK 1	WEEK 2	WEEK 3	WEEK 4	WEEK 5
2 × Swim (2)	2 × Swim (2)	2 × Swim (2/3)	2 × Swim (2/3)	2 × Swim (2/3)
2 × Bike (2)	2 × Bike (2)	2 × Bike (one at 3, one at 2)	2 × Bike (2/3)	2 × Bike (2/3)
1 × Run (2)	1 × Run (2)	2 × Run (2)	2 × Run (2)	2 × Run (2)
2 × Strength	2 × Strength	2 × Strength	2 × Strength	2 × Strength
Week 1 of the training programme starts with some low intensity sessions, getting your body used to a structured training programme	Week 2 continues the steady start of the previous week	Week 3 increases distance and intensity levels	Week 4 continues adding distance to all three disciplines	Week 5 continues a similar profile to Week 4
Swim – 2 swim sessions including drills and easy swimming		Swim – start including some interval sessions with zone 3 efforts	Swim – intervals should be continued but increased in length	
Bike – steady riding		Bike – one of the bike rides should include some intervals or hill repeats at a higher intensity	Bike – the long bike ride should increase to 150mins. The shorter ride should include some intervals or hill reps	
Run – 1 easy run		Run – an extra run is introduced but both are at an easy pace	Run – The long run should be at 90mins	
Week Totals:	Week Totals:	Week Totals:	Week Totals:	Week Totals:
Swim – 3km	Swim – 3.5km	Swim – 4km	Swim – 4.5km	Swim – 4.5km
Bike – 150mins	Bike – 180mins	Bike – 210mins	Bike – 240mins	Bike – 240mins
Run – 60mins	Run – 60mins	Run – 120mins	Run – 150mins	Run – 150mins

Table 11.7 Base Phase Training Schedule (continued)

WEEK 6	WEEK 7	WEEK 8	WEEK 9	WEEK 10
2 × Swim (2) 1 × Bike (2) 1 × Run (2) 2 × Strength	3 × Swim (2/3) 2 × Bike (2/3) 2 × Run (2) 2–3 × Strength	3 × Swim (2/3) 2 × Bike (2/3) 2 × Run (2) 2–3 × Strength	3 × Swim (2/3) 2 × Bike (2/3) 2 × Run (2) 2–3 × Strength	2 × Swim (2) 2 × Bike (2) 1 × Run (2) 1 × Core Strength
Intensity and distance is reduced as this week acts as a much easier one. Ensure you take 2–3 days off during the week	Week 7 – steps up again in distance and intensity of sessions	Week 8 continues the intensity and distances of Week 7	The long bike and run sessions are increased in distance again	After some hard weeks, Week 10 is a rest week and all sessions should be of a low intensity
Swim – 2 very easy swims Bike – a 3-hour easy bike ride Run – one run of 105mins	Swim – an extra swim session is included this week. Keep a mix between long and short intervals, maintaining drills Bike – the long bike ride should increase to 180mins. The shorter ride should include some intervals or hill reps Run – the long run is increased to 120mins		Swim – increase one swim session up to 3km, keep the second session as an interval session and the third an easy swim Bike – the long bike is increased to 4hrs at an easy pace. Include some intervals or hill reps in the second session Run – the long run is increased to 135mins	Swim – 2 easy swim sessions, include a 3-km non-stop easy effort Bike – a long 4-hr easy bike is maintained, but reduce if you don't feel you are recovering from the week Run – a long easy run is maintained, but, as per the bike, if you feel tired reduce this in length
Week Totals: Swim – 4km Bike – 180mins Run – 105mins	Week Totals: Swim –7km Bike – 330mins Run – 210mins	Week Totals: Swim – 7km Bike – 330mins Run – 210mins	Week Totals: Swim – 7.5km Bike – 360mins Run – 225mins	Week Totals: Swim –5km Bike – 300mins Run – 150mins

Table 11.8 Build Phase Training Schedule

WEEK 11	WEEK 12	WEEK 13	WEEK 14	WEEK 15
3 × Swim (3) 2 × Bike (2/3) 3 × Run (including one brick run) (2) 2–3 × Strength	3 × Swim (3) 2 × Bike (2/3) 3 × Run (including one brick run) (2) 2–3 × Strength	2 × Swim (2) 2 × Bike (2/3) 2 × Run (2) 2–3 × Strength	3 × Swim (3) 2 × Bike (2/3) 3 × Run (including one brick run) (2/3) 2 × Strength	3 × Swim (3) 2 × Bike (2/3) 3 × Run (including one brick run) (2/3) 2 × Strength
The beginning of the build phase includes the first brick session. The long ride and run are also increased in length	This week sees a slight increase in distance again. Some race pace riding is also included in your long ride	A rest week. If you do not feel you are recovering, reduce these efforts further or take extra rest days instead	A tough week, distances are increased on the bike as well as for swimming	This week is similar to last week except the long run is increased in distance
Swim – 3 swim interval sessions (2 at 3kms) Bike – a long ride of 4hrs and a shorter higher intensity ride including intervals or hill reps Run – the first brick run, 15mins off the shorter bike ride. A longer run of 2–2.5hrs and a mid-distance steady run should also be included.	Swim – similar to last week, although one swim is increased to 3.5km Bike – one high intensity session and a 4-hr ride including 5 × 15mins of roughly race pace riding Run – keep the long run of 2–2.5hrs. For the second run try a 1.5-hr run including the final 45mins at your standalone marathon pace. Keep the brick run the same as last week.	Swim – 2 easy swims with drills Bike – a long ride at an easy pace and a slightly faster 90-min ride focusing on good form Run – 2 easy runs, with the long run reduced to 90mins	Swim – 2 swim interval sessions and an endurance swim of 3.5km Bike – the long bike is increased to 5hrs, with an additional 2.5-hr ride in the week, including intervals Run – if you are comfortably coping with the running sessions, run your mid-distance session at a slightly faster tempo pace	Swim – similar to last week Bike – similar to last week Run – the long run is increased to 2.5hrs if you are capable
Week Totals: Swim – 8.5km Bike – 360mins Run – 270mins	Week Totals: Swim – 9km Bike – 360mins Run – 285mins	Week Totals: Swim – 4.5km Bike – 210mins Run – 150mins	Week Totals: Swim – 9km Bike – 450mins Run – 255mins	Week Totals: Swim – 9km Bike – 450mins Run – 255mins

Table 11.8 Build Phase Training Schedule (continued)

WEEK 16	WEEK 17	WEEK 18	WEEK 19	WEEK 20
2 × Swim (2)	3 × Swim (3)	3 × Swim (3)	2 × Swim (2)	3 × Swim (3)
2 × Bike (2/3)	2 × Bike (2/3)	2 × Bike (2/3)	2 × Bike (2)	2 × Bike (2/3)
2 × Run (2)	3 × Run (including one brick run) (2/3)	3 × Run (including one brick run) (2/3)	3 × Run (including one brick run) (2/3)	3 × Run (including one brick run) (2/3)
1 × Strength	2 × Strength	2 × Strength	1 × Strength	2 × Strength
A rest week. If you do not feel you are recovering, reduce these efforts further or take extra rest days instead	Another tough week! Swim – the endurance swim is increased to 4km Bike – if you are comfortably riding the long ride, start to include some faster pace efforts (for example 4 × 20mins at zone 3) Run – maintain the tempo run, long run and brick session	Swim – take the second swim of the week quite easy in preparation for a 3.8-km time trial for the third swim (if possible in a wetsuit in open water) Bike – maintain a similar schedule to last week Run – if the long run is comfortable, include 3 × 20mins of slightly faster running (stand-alone marathon pace)	A rest week. If you do not feel you are recovering, reduce these efforts further or take extra rest days instead	One of the last high-volume weeks. Swim – the 4-km distance session is maintained
Swim – 2 easy swims with drills Bike – a medium ride at an easy pace and a slightly faster 90-min ride focusing on good form Run – 2 easy runs, with the long run reduced to 90mins			Swim – 2 easy swims with drills Bike – a medium ride at an easy pace and a slightly faster 90-min ride focusing on good form Run – 2 easy runs, with the long run reduced to 90mins and a short run off the longer bike ride	Bike – include some race pace efforts in the long bike ride (for example 4 × 20mins at race pace) Run – keep the tempo run, long run with faster efforts and brick session going
Week Totals: Swim – 5km Bike – 210mins Run – 150mins	Week Totals: Swim – 9.5km Bike – 450mins Run – 270mins	Week Totals: Swim – 9.5km Bike – 450mins Run – 285mins	Week Totals: Swim – 5km Bike – 240mins Run – 165mins	Week Totals: Swim – 9.5km Bike – 450mins Run – 315mins

Table 11.9 Peak Phase Training Schedule

WEEK 21	WEEK 22	WEEK 23
3 × Swim (3) 2 × Bike (2/3) 2 × Run (2/3) 1 × Strength	2 × Swim (3) 2 × Bike (2/3) 3 × Run (including one brick run) (2/3) 1 × Strength	2 × Swim (2/3) 2 × Bike (2) 2 × Run (3/4)
Volume is starting to reduce with some higher quality sharpener sessions being included	Volume is reduced again and the higher intensity maintained. If you are feeling tired in the week, reduce distances of sessions substantially	No fitness gains to be had this week, just keep the body ticking over and rested
Swim – introduce some shorter, faster intervals and start reducing overall length of swims Bike – start reducing length of the long ride and increase the intensity of the rides Run – last long run before the race, start freshening the legs with some shorter tempo runs	Swim – same as previous week, but with one less swim Bike – a steady medium length ride and a shorter tempo ride Run – longest run reduced to 90mins, a short, fast tempo run (around 45–60mins) and a short run off the bike should leave you starting to feel fresh	Swim – 2 easy swims with drills Bike – 2 easy short rides Run – 2 easy runs
Week Totals: Swim – 8.0km Bike – 270mins Run – 210mins	Week Totals: Swim – 8.0km Bike – 270mins Run – 195mins	Week Totals: Swim – 4.5km Bike – 150mins Run – 105mins

RACE WEEK – ONE WEEK

>> **Swim:** No more than two swims in race week, just to keep your shoulders and arms engaged. If it's possible, one swim in the race venue would give you a feel for the water.

>> **Bike/run:** One or two easy rides/runs to keep the body ready for race day.

Table 11.10 Race Week Training Schedule

WEEK 24
2 × Swim (2) 1 × Bike (2) 1 × Run (1)
The goal this week is to keep resting but also to keep ticking over so your body is ready for race day.
Swim – 2 short swims so the body doesn't lose the feel of the water Bike – short ride, normally riding a part of the race course Run – an easy jog to keep the legs engaged
Week Totals: Swim – 2km Bike – 60mins Run – 20–40mins

TOTAL RACE PLAN SUMMARY

Set out below are the training distances and times summarised from the plans above. The maximum amount of training in a week amounts to approximately 16 hours, while the average for the period is just over ten hours. This level of training is not necessary to complete a long-distance triathlon or indeed to do well in one. Some people thrive on heavy training weeks (plus 20-hour weeks) while others can do 10–15 hours and put in impressive performances. Often these people have an existing high fitness endurance base built over several years of training, which just needs maintaining. But don't get hung up on the number of hours you are training, just get the key sessions done and keep a consistent level of training which builds the endurance and, for some sessions, the intensity.

Figure 11.1: Training Hours Per Week

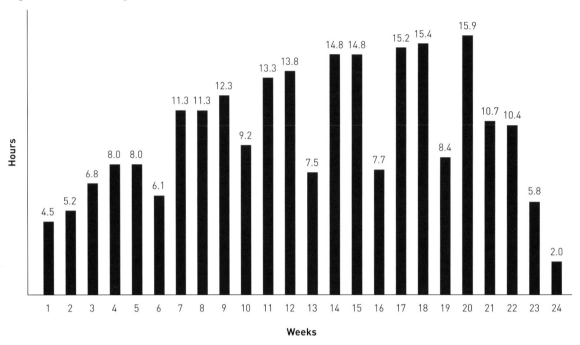

Figure 11.2: Swim Plan Summary (weekly swim totals in kms)

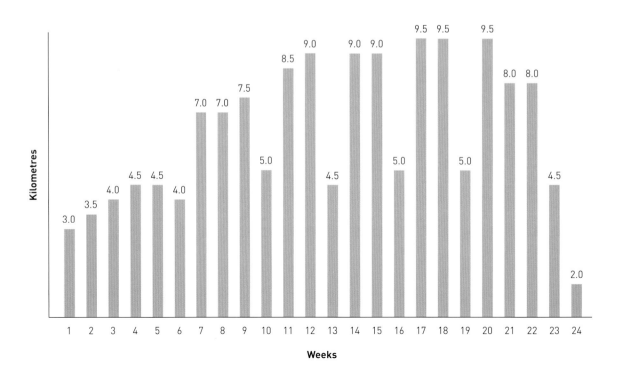

Figure 11.3: Bike Plan Summary (weekly bike totals in mins)

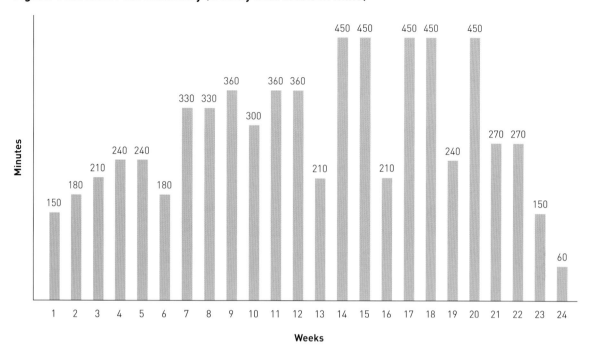

Figure 11.4: Run Plan Summary (weekly run totals in mins)

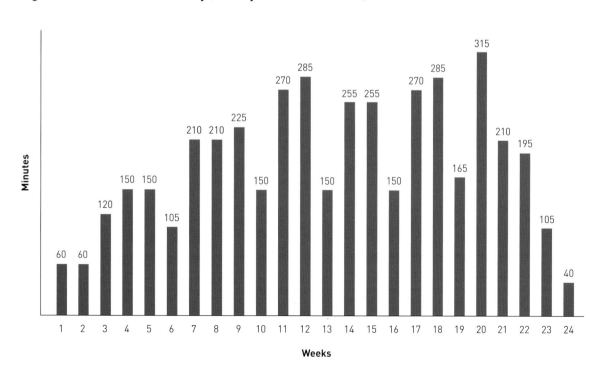

CHAPTER 012:
THE TAPER_

'The principle is competing against yourself. It's about self-improvement, about being better than you were the day before.'

– Steve Young, Former American Football Player

THE LAST THREE weeks before the race is a period known as the taper. Tapering for any triathlon is tricky. There are a number of reasons for this. First, a lot of people aren't really sure what they should do during a taper. And second, when you've spent anywhere from three months upwards pushing your body to extremes, dramatically reducing the amount of training that you are doing can feel quite strange.

But tapering – like so many aspects of triathlon training – is essential. It is your body's opportunity to rest, recover and be ready to take on one of the toughest tasks in sport. And like any part of long-distance triathlons, it needs to be carefully scheduled into your routine.

Of course, in the final week before a race, reduced exercise and plenty of rest should be your focus. But the body needs more than a week to recover and repair itself, and your taper period should begin at least three weeks before the race.

In this chapter we are going to look at three different aspects of the taper in the build-up to race day. These are your training intensity, your nutrition/hydration and the importance of massages. All of them play key roles in getting you ready for race day.

Needless to say, rest is essential as well. We don't include a section on resting here, but to get your body in prime shape you need to do as little as possible in

the hours you've put aside for resting and relaxing. Just because you aren't spending Saturday morning sitting on your bike for six hours doesn't mean you have six-hours to build a new house or something similar. Rest, relax, and let your body recover.

TRAINING

As we have already said, a lot of people have a lot of problems with the taper. People often fall into one of two traps: going completely cold turkey, or training hard up until two to three days before the event.

While the former will probably mean that you don't feel too sharp on race day, the latter is undoubtedly less effective. However, the key is to find the right balance for you. Some people find that a six-hour bike takes a lot out of them. Others find that they can do a six-hour bike one day and feel fresh enough to run upwards of 30 kilometres the next. Everyone is different. You know how your body responds to the training and you know how much time it takes you to recover.

The following guide is for someone who might be deemed 'typical'. They don't recover quickly, nor does it take days and days for them to get over their training. They are fit, healthy, comfortable doing the long rides but are by no means a genetic freak who can recover in the blink of an eye.

Three Weeks To Go

If you are our typical person, your taper in earnest should start three weeks before the race. That doesn't mean you are going to stop training three weeks out from the race, but that you are gradually going to start winding down the amount of bike and run training that you are doing.

In particular, you should stop your long run and ride sessions, from which the body can take the longest time to recover. The focus instead should be on tempo sessions, which allow you to sharpen up and come away from a session feeling energised, rather than completely worn out. This week might be a good opportunity for a final shorter brick session, using your

race kit and nutrition, acting as a dress rehearsal for the race itself.

However, you should aim to keep your regular swim sessions, again with the emphasis on 'shorter and faster' rather than long intervals. As swimming is non-weight-bearing, recovery is usually a lot quicker than biking and running, so it's possible to keep fairly intense sessions up until race week.

Two Weeks To Go

Again, the training volume should be reduced and you should be finishing sessions feeling energised, fresh and strong. If you're not feeling like that, look to take time off completely from exercise. As with the first

One Week To Go

Any sessions this week are designed to keep you 'ticking over' and race ready. Doing any intense training will only have a detrimental impact on race day. Ideally, you will swim at least two or three times during this last week. Keep the sessions short. You will have bursts of race pace swimming in there, but the main aim is to maintain the feel for the water.

Two easy runs in the week of no more than 30 minutes – including plenty of stretching – will help keep your legs in good form. A couple of bike rides of an hour will have the same result. Usually the Friday before a Sunday race will involve a short swim and then a complete rest on Saturday.

But this is where it really comes down to you. How do you feel? Listen to your body. You will have nervous energy in there that makes you feel lethargic and the chances are you'll suddenly feel niggles and aches that you didn't feel before. Often that is your mind playing tricks on you. You know how you feel and you know what you are capable of doing. If you are tired, take some time off (you have earned it). But ideally, you want to be keeping your training ticking over.

Massages

Some people swear by them, others have never had one, but the simple fact is that a sports massage can do wonders for your weary limbs.

A couple of weeks before your race, it is definitely worth investing in a massage. It will help to stretch out the muscles and give your legs and back (in particular) a bit of TLC.

But don't make the mistake of booking your first massage a few days before the event. If your body is not used to a massage, you may find that you end up with more aches and pains post massage than you had when you went in. That is why you want to get a nice, easy 'rub down' seven to ten days before the race. If you find it beneficial, by all means get more in the build-up to race day.

week of the taper, sessions should be short and fast, with the aim of bringing your body to its peak in time for the race.

This week try and include 20 minutes of stretching every day (if you're not already doing that) and maybe look into getting a sports massage. The massage will indicate any remaining areas of stiffness and assist in preparing muscles to be in optimum condition.

Ensure you are getting as much sleep as possible and try and avoid as much other stress as possible. You should be relaxing your body and preparing your mind for the race ahead.

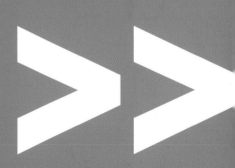

PART 04:
KEEPING YOUR
BODY IN SHAPE_

CHAPTER 013
NUTRITION AND HYDRATION_

'Nutrition and hydration play a huge part in every race. It does come down to planning but also practice in training. However, you also need to use your brain on race day as you need to take into conderation the conditions, the temperature, wind, how you're feeling, the effort you're putting out...'

– Bella Bayliss, Fifteen-Time Ironman Champion

YOU CAN PRACTISE swimming, cycling and running as much as you like, but the simple truth of long-distance triathlon racing is that if you don't fuel correctly during the race you probably won't finish. In fact, getting your nutrition and hydration strategy right is essential to ensuring that you have a successful race.

By the time the gun goes off you should know exactly how you are going to fuel during the race and have practised that strategy. Admittedly, the best-laid plans do not always come to fruition and you cannot account for every variable on race day, but you still need to make that plan.

During the course of a long-distance triathlon you can expect to burn anything up to 10,000 calories. You might even burn more than that. Somehow, you need to work out how you are going to replace the majority of fluid and energy that is expended during the eight hours and upwards that you will be racing. And unless

you have a stomach of steel, don't necessarily expect your body to tolerate energy gels and bars for the duration of the race.

This chapter is a basic introduction to fuelling, hydration and diet. However, it cannot tell you how to fuel your race. Everyone is different – some people need a lot of food just to help them survive a day sitting in an office, some people eat hardly anything. What you need to do is use the information included here, and apply it during your training sessions to find out what works for you.

MANAGING YOUR DIET

Although it is sometimes overlooked, managing your diet during training for a long-distance triathlon is extremely important. The increase in volume and intensity of your training sessions are going to have a noticeable impact on your body's needs.

What you cannot afford to do during this period is fail to adjust your diet accordingly. You are going to be burning a lot more calories than you have probably ever done before, and your immune system is going to be placed under high levels of stress.

Weight-wise, do not be afraid of dropping a few kilograms (every triathlete aspires towards their 'race weight'). But make sure that you keep an eye on it. Some people find that they lose too much weight in the build-up to a long-distance triathlon. As well as having a detrimental impact on athletic performance, drastic weight loss can make an athlete more susceptible to illness, and even lead to severe physical complications.

In terms of your immune system, you need to ensure that you are eating a healthy, balanced diet. Under stress, the body tends to maintain a high level of immunity to compensate for the stress. But during periods of 'down time' (tapering, for instance) your levels of immunity will actually drop. A healthy, balanced diet will help to compensate for this drop and ensure that you have the best possible chance of feeling on top form come race day.

To ensure that you are fuelling healthily, your diet needs to contain a good mix of the following:

Carbohydrate

What is it? Carbohydrate is basically sugar that your body converts into glucose, which becomes your main source of energy. There are two types of carbohydrate: simple and complex. Simple carbohydrates are quick and easy to digest, while complex carbohydrates are more difficult. This means that simple carbs get into your system much faster than complex carbs (which are generally considered to be a form of slow-release energy).

Why do I need it? It's your main source of energy during middle and high intensity training.

Where can I find it? Everywhere! You can get simple carbs naturally in fruit and vegetables and in refined form in foods such as biscuits, cakes, chocolate, soft drinks, and sweets. Complex carbs, meanwhile, can be found in pasta, potatoes, brown rice, brown bread, bagels, wheat-based cereals, oat-based cereals, peas, beans, porridge.

What should I eat? The more refined the carbohydrate the faster glucose is released into your blood, leading to peaks and troughs in your energy levels. Conversely, the slower the release of glucose into the body the more sustainable and stable your energy levels will be. So try eating fibre wholegrain cereals and wholemeal toast for breakfast. Base your main meal around a complex carbohydrate along with vegetables and finish off with fruit. This will provide a balance of both complex and simple carbohydrates.

While racing and training for longer periods at a medium to high level of intensity carbohydrate will be your main energy source. If you do not replenish this carbohydrate you will run out of energy with an obviously large negative impact on your performance – this is often known as 'hitting the wall'.

Protein

What is it? Without going into the ins-and-outs of amino acids, protein makes up your muscles, hair, skin, bones etc. And the body doesn't find it easy to store protein, which means it needs to be 'topped up' regularly.

Why do I need it? When you are training, your body breaks down the muscle tissue (which is one of the reasons why you feel stiff). Protein rebuilds that muscle tissue and also helps optimise carbohydrate storage. It is also a secondary source of energy.

Where can I find it? In many foods including, eggs, milk, chicken, fish, cheese, yoghurt, meat in general (in varying quantities), cereals, beans and nuts.

Fat

What is it? Pretty much everything you eat that is grown on Mother Earth has some sort of natural fat in it, and it's good for you – in limited quantities. However, a breakdown of the number of different fats shows that some are better for you than others:

>> **Saturated fats:** These natural fats are OK in limited doses and are found, for example, in meat, butter and cheese. In excessive doses this type of fat can raise cholesterol levels and increase your risk of many chronic diseases.

>> **Unsaturated fats:** These natural fats are good for you and can be found in oily fish, avocados, unsalted nuts and seeds. Unsaturated fats contain essential fatty acids that cannot be made by the body and so we need to get them from foods.

>> **Trans fats:** These are predominantly man-made and found in processed foods. They can raise cholesterol levels and increase your risk of many chronic diseases; they should be minimised as much as possible.

Why do I need it? Fat provides the main fuel source for long duration, low-intensity exercise. When you exercise above this level of intensity, you will be using mainly carbohydrates as your energy source.

It takes the body a long time to digest and convert fat into a usable form of energy, or indeed break down stored fat into a usable form of energy. Fat is needed to help access the stored carbohydrate for higher intensity exercise and has a number of other uses such as keeping your organs healthy.

A healthy diet will help your performance overall. By eating natural, healthy foodstuffs, you are automatically giving your body the vitamins, minerals and energy that it needs to perform to the level you are asking. It is also giving it the food that it needs to fight off infections and illnesses, and will help stop you from feeling lethargic all of the time (which can happen when your training reaches its peak).

EATING FREQUENCY

When you start training, you might find that you get hungry quite frequently. That is particularly the case if you start putting early morning swims into your routine. The mantra at this point is 'little and often'. If you can develop a diet that allows you to eat smaller 'meals' up to six times a day, you will find that you will be able to maintain a healthy weight and sustain an intensive training routine. See box below for a sample eating plan.

SAMPLE EATING PLAN

Breakfast: Fibre wholegrain cereals, wholemeal bread and fruit, yoghurt

Mid-morning snack: Bagel, unsalted nuts

Lunch: Large carbohydrate meals can make you feel sluggish, so choose a lean protein meal such as fish or chicken with only a small amount of carbohydrate and add salad or vegetables

Mid-afternoon snack: Unsalted nuts, fruit, yoghurt

Pre-training snack: Fruit

Supper: Based around a complex carbohydrate (such as pasta or brown rice), with vegetables, salad and protein

Remember, the above eating plan is just a guide. Not everyone needs to eat this much while others need to eat more. The key is to make sure that you are not hungry and that you maintain a healthy diet that keeps your energy levels up. You are using up enough of your carbohydrate supplies when you are training; do not try and burn them out when you are doing your day-to-day tasks as well.

A WORD ON ALCOHOL

There are a thousand and one different opinions about alcohol and athletic performance. In reality though, alcohol dehydrates you, impairs your reaction time, impacts your body's ability to process amino acids and impedes your ability to train effectively. It is also a depressant.

However, long-distance triathlon training doesn't have to impact on your social life. Sure, alcohol isn't great for training and by all means cut it out of your diet if you want to. But don't feel that you have to. You will see plenty of long-distance triathlon competitors having a few beers post race (and you might even see some of them having a beer during the race). Remember this is a hobby. It's a very time-intensive hobby, but a hobby nonetheless. Don't let it take away from the things that you enjoy doing.

However, don't plan a key training session the morning after a night out drinking, and in the run-up to race day it makes sense to restrict or stop drinking altogether.

FUELLING FOR TRAINING AND RACING

While all athletes need to maintain a good diet, as a long-distance triathlete you need to pay particular attention to periods of heavy training and of course, on race day, when pre-race eating will not be sufficient in providing you with the energy to make it to the finish. As you will be engaged in activity at a moderate to sometimes high intensity, your primary energy source will be carbohydrates which, although stored naturally in the muscles, may only last for around two hours of exercise (and so need to be topped up during exercise). You will also need to consider replacing minerals, such as sodium and magnesium, to keep your body functioning and not cramping up.

The good news is that there is a whole industry dedicated to providing carbohydrate- and electrolyte-rich products that will provide the fuel for your training and the race itself. There is also a range of other natural alternatives to try which we will come on to in due course. The bad news is that there is no simple prescription for this and it is only through trial and error, product-testing and hard work that you will be able to work out what is the best fuelling strategy for you.

Carbohydrate and Electrolyte Replacement

Energy and electrolyte replacement products are available in the form of energy drinks (already made or in powder form to be diluted), energy bars, energy gels and others such as energy jellies and jelly beans. As you will no doubt have seen, there is a dizzying selection of brands available in bicycle and triathlon shops these days and they've even started to make their way into chemists and supermarkets. Below is a guide to help you get started in understanding the purpose of each product and when it could be used.

Synthetic foodstuffs

Gels

Energy gels come in small sachets that can be ripped open as you cycle or run and sucked down. Taste and constitution varies from a thick, treacle-like substance to something a little more diluted, depending on the brand you try. Most contain around 500kj of energy (120 calories) and should be taken every 30–45 minutes during exercise. Try a few different brands and flavours – hopefully you will find one that you can keep down. If you're lucky it might even taste good!

Some gels include caffeine. This additional caffeine will give you a more immediate 'hit' of energy which could be useful if you are going through a bad patch, or nearing the end of the run when you are going flat out to the finish.

Bars

Much like gels, bars are designed to replace your carbohydrate energy reserves (a standard bar will contain 600–900kj of energy or 140–220 calories), although as they are solid they should provide a longer period of energy release. They will often include additional minerals. However, most importantly, they provide real food for your stomach, which is most likely to be awash with liquid. This can be important for your fuelling strategy (and something you should experiment with) because your body might start to reject a constant succession of gels every half hour over an eight hour plus day. Many people aim to eat a couple of bars during the bike section, when your heart rate is lower and your body can digest solid foods more easily, which gives you time to benefit from the slower release of energy.

Another advantage of eating bars when training or racing is that you can abide by the mantra 'little and often' by just taking regular bites. Once opened a gel has to be fully consumed or discarded.

Like gels, the taste and constitution of bars varies wildly from brand to brand. Some of them are full of chocolate, others of oats and nuts; some are very dry,

others are quite sticky. As with everything, only you know which type you prefer and it is worth trying out a few different brands to see which is best for you.

Jelly beans/energy jellies

With a similar profile to energy gels, jelly beans and energy jellies offer another method of giving your body the energy it needs. Often more tasty and palatable than gels or even bars, they are becoming a more common sight in shops and are definitely worth with a try.

Non-synthetic foodstuffs

In an ideal world you'd get all of the energy you need for a triathlon out of food of the non-synthetic variety. Unfortunately, in terms of effective energy delivery, ease of use and practicality, specifically designed synthetic products offer several advantages.

But there are some natural products that are worth considering.

>> **Bananas:** A great source of both energy and potassium, bananas are an invaluable training aid. Chop them in half (so they're easily accessible) and eat them in the first 90 minutes of a ride (or eat one prior to exercise). Most long-distance triathlons will give them out at feed stations and they can be a good way of giving your stomach the 'solid' food it may need.

>> **Raisins:** An average packet of raisins actually packs as much punch as an energy gel (around 500kj). Although less practical to eat when exercising and they will take longer for the body to convert into energy, they are a good natural alternative.

>> **Sticky raisin buns:** A bun with raisins can provide a more tasty long-term energy source for your long training rides and is also a tasty alternative to synthetic foodstuffs.

Energy drinks/water

There are numerous sports drinks on the market that help keep you hydrated, and like the products listed above 'top up' your energy reserves and electrolyte intake. Make sure you choose products that are designed to provide carbohydrate and electrolytes and again you need to find the flavour that works best for you.

Getting the balance of energy drink and water right takes time and experience. Some people can easily stomach bottles of energy drink without any negative effect, while others will find this makes them nauseous. Balance your intake, but ensure you are drinking enough and not just waiting until you feel thirsty. Set a timescale for what you will drink and when; for example, take small mouthfuls every ten minutes and aim to drink 750ml every 45 minutes.

WIND DOWN FROM TRAINING, WIND UP FOR THE RACE

As you wind down your training, you should be looking to wind up your focus on nutrition and hydration. But to get those two things right requires an entirely different approach to the age-old carb-loading myth.

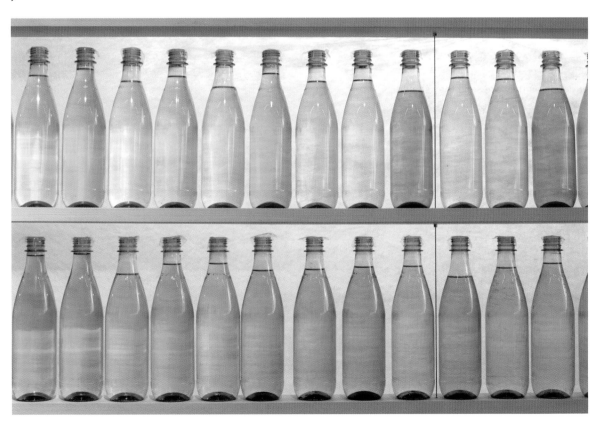

Instead, at the start of the week leading up to the race, you should be focusing on proteins and fats (not the deep fried sort). Of course, you need carbohydrate in there, but this will help you to build up a more balanced energy reserve. What's more, because you are reducing the amount of exercise you are doing, you will build a calorie surplus.

Two to three days before the race is the time to start focusing on carbohydrates. Don't go ballistic on the stuff, but keep it steady and keep it coming. As per your normal diet, your body will respond better if you eat little and often. When we say little, though, we don't mean tiny. You want to be eating slightly more than your usual amount of carbohydrate, but you don't want to be bloated.

The Carb-Loading Myth

When most people start doing triathlon, someone somewhere tells them that before a race they need to carb-load. So logic suggests that before a long-distance triathlon you should carb-load to the max. The theory behind this is that if you spend days building up your stores of glycogen, your body will have more to consume on race day.

Unfortunately, this is something of a myth. Various scientific experiments have demonstrated that the body is only capable of storing up enough glycogen to take it through two to two-and-a-half hours of high intensity work. In fact, a week of carb-loading can actually be detrimental to your physiology and subsequent performance.

As well as storing fuel, your body can also store salt. And you're going to need salt. Again, everything in moderation, but it is worth making sure that you are taking on salt to replace what you will inevitably lose.

Finally, on race day morning stick with what you know. Of course, eat a little bit more than you normally would for breakfast, but don't try anything new. Make sure you eat your race day breakfast a few hours before the start of the race, giving your body enough time to digest what you are putting into it.

Hydrated and Ready to Go

The human body isn't a simple thing to hydrate. If you're dehydrated it can take days to bring your body up to 'normal' levels of hydration. And that is why you need to have a pre-race hydration plan in place. Don't worry; it's not like your race plan. Instead, it's simply a matter of remembering to drink regularly.

It is quite difficult to know how much water/energy drink you need to consume to compensate for what you lose. But the simplest way of working this out is to weigh yourself pre- and post-exercise. You'll need to be naked (or as good as) in both instances, and you need to weigh yourself within 15 minutes of completing your training session. If 1kg equals 1000ml, you can calculate how much you have lost compared to how much you have put in, and therefore how much you need to be drinking during a training session.

This calculation will give you a basic idea of the weight you lose through sweat during a session. Putting a large quantity of that back in is key. Whether that is through energy drinks or water, you may find that you need to consume up to 1–1.5 litres per hour if training in warm weather.

The average person needs to drink 2.5 litres a day (that's about 4.5 pints). And that doesn't include tea or coffee. But remember, when you're training you are not an 'average' person. On top of drinking the 'average' amount of water, you need to compensate for fluid loss from training sessions in the taper weeks.

Don't go over the top on fluid intake though (hyponatremia can kill you if you go too far), but do make sure you are drinking a good amount so come race day you are hydrated and ready to go.

THE RACE

It isn't possible to overstate the importance of using your training sessions to formulate a nutrition and hydration plan for the race. Of course, you have to be flexible with this plan and respond to the various variables that confront you on race day. But if you have a basic plan in place, you have a much better chance of making it to the finishing line in your target time.

Pre-Race Nutrition

It goes without saying that in the build-up to a long-distance triathlon you need to be eating well. This is particularly true in the last week, when your body will start to build up energy supplies and you should be hydrating (dehydration is cumulative and so you cannot just re-hydrate over the course of 24 hours).

In the final few days, focus on foods that are high in carbohydrates and easy to digest, such as pasta, fruits, vegetables and breads. On the morning of the race, you should again eat a breakfast that is high in carbohydrates but, most importantly, is easy to digest. Practise your race breakfast several times before training sessions and don't be tempted to experiment on race day! Try wholemeal toast and fruit, but be careful of taking dairy products as these can sit in your stomach and cause problems when you start racing. Following breakfast you will often have 2–3 hours before the start of the race, so try eating a banana or energy bar during this period while keeping hydrated with water or an energy drink.

The Swim

There are people who take a gel on the swim. It's difficult to know how they manage to do it, but there are a number of people who do. If you find the swim leg particularly exhausting, try tucking a gel into the arm of your wetsuit and then find an opportune moment to

take it (although be careful that you don't get mown down by the rest of the field). For most people though, nutrition during the swim is not necessary.

The Bike

This is where you have to get your nutrition and hydration right and the leg where your fuelling plan can be executed in a controlled manner. The bike will also allow you to eat solid foods (which might not be possible on the run), and so complete the race with 'proper' food in your stomach.

Aim for 200–500 calories and up to 1,000mg of sodium an hour on the bike, sourced from any of the products discussed above. If you are using solid foods, start with these and progress on to gels and energy drinks. Drink up to 1.5 litres of water and/or energy drink an hour, using water after eating or taking gels to aid digestion. Your actual intake will depend on a range of factors not limited to your size, fitness or how hot the day is. Again you will have practised this in training and will know what works best for you.

AID STATIONS ON THE BIKE WILL NORMALLY PROVIDE:

>> Energy bars and gels (usually from a sponsored partner, find out who this is so you can try their products before race day)

>> Energy drinks (again from a sponsored partner)

>> Water

>> Bananas

>> Flat Coke

In addition to this you can normally submit a special needs pack that you can pick up halfway around the bike course and include in there any specific foods or drinks you might need.

Try and maintain a systematic and frequent approach to taking on fluids and nutrition; if it helps set your watch to beep every 15–20 minutes as a reminder to eat or drink.

The Run

Fuelling on the run can be tricky. Your body is exhausted and your stomach may be sick of gels or energy drink. Fortunately, aid stations on the run usually have a wider variation of foodstuffs (check the race website for details), which could include:

>> Energy bars

>> Energy gels

>> Nuts

>> Fruit

>> Sweets

>> Salted products (often pretzels)

>> Bananas

>> Energy drinks

>> Flat Coke

>> Water

To help set you up for the run, take it easy or walk through the first couple of aid stations to get enough food on board. Again, there is the opportunity to submit a special needs bag, which may prove of benefit halfway through the run.

Most of your energy during the run will likely come from gels and energy drinks. Buying a belt in which to keep your nutrition while running can be useful if you don't want to take the gels offered at the aid stations. Try taking a gel (or bag of energy jellies/jelly beans) every 20 minutes whilst running and eat how you feel regarding other foodstuffs. Even if you don't feel hungry, keep your calorie intake high to ensure you don't hit the wall later on in the race. If you feel you are becoming irritable or depressed, you may be suffering from low blood sugar and so a few handfuls of sweets or a swig of Coke can make you feel more positive.

You may get to a point when your body craves something in particular – this is when you have to start eating as you feel. Slow down through aid stations and take on what you feel you need. Often gels and energy drink will be hard to keep down, so switch to other products on offer.

Recovery

When the training session or the race is finished your body still needs to recover. Do not overlook the importance of recovery drinks to help this process. Find a recovery drink that has a high concentration of carbohydrates, protein, and sodium, and which as a bonus also tastes nice. This will help your muscles recover, and replace some of the minerals and energy that have been taken out of your body. To be effective, recovery drinks should be consumed within 20 minutes of the end of your exercise period.

There is a non-synthetic product that does work effectively as a recovery drink – full-fat milk. While it doesn't have everything that sports drinks have, it does have a high concentration of protein that will help feed your muscles and so expedite recovery.

>> CHAPTER 014:
KEEPING YOU ON THE ROAD TO RACE DAY_

'Who me? I never get fatigued. Yeah, I wish. As any triathlete knows it is a constant battle between pushing the envelope by training and racing hard, and getting enough recovery.'

– Julie Dibens, Ironman 70.3 Champion, Third 2010 Ironman World Championships

KEEPING YOURSELF ON the road to race day is much easier said than done. There are a whole host of factors that will influence your ability – and condition – on the start line come race day.

It's a simple fact that best intentions are not good enough for long-distance triathlon racing. Both the training and race will be incredibly tough on your body. What's more, just because you've entered doesn't mean that you have a right to finish. A lot of people don't make the cut-off time, some will retire injured or exhausted during the race, and a large number won't even make it to race day.

Which is where this chapter comes in. Because long-distance triathlon racing is so much more than 10, 12, 15 or 17 hours of physical exertion. It is the days, weeks and months leading up to the race. It is the blood, sweat and tears. And it is the potential for injuries that run hand in hand with one of the toughest sports on the planet.

DEALING WITH INJURIES

Before we begin, it is important to note we're not doctors. Nor are we physiotherapists for that matter. If you suffer from repeat or severe injuries, go and see a doctor or a physio. Because of the unique design of the human body, no two injuries are ever quite the same, and so the information provided below is little more than a basic overview.

The first note of caution is to be aware of the temptation to try and train through an injury. It is easy to become so fixated on your training that you decide to push on, no matter what. Don't. This is when a small problem can turn into something much more serious, which in turn can mean that you will miss more than just a couple of training sessions. If you feel a small tweak or strain developing, it is at first worth considering the acronym RICE.

RICE stands for *R*est, *I*ce, *C*ompression and *E*levation, and is a well-versed solution to many common triathlon injuries. Of course, it won't solve everything. But it is a good starting point for some of the more regular complaints made by triathletes.

But what are these more common complaints? Well, a lot of triathletes will experience at least one (and hopefully not more) of the following during their preparation for a long-distance triathlon race:

>> **Runner's knee:** Patellofemoral pain syndrome is probably the most common running injury. You'll know if you have runner's knee. It starts with a dull pain below the kneecap, which gets progressively more painful the more you run on it. If you try to run through it, you may find that the pain is not just limited to running, but can also be felt when resting, too.

>> **Achilles tendonitis:** Another very common complaint, Achilles tendonitis is caused by a swelling on the Achilles tendon. Sufferers will usually experience pain either above or around the heel when they begin exercising. This pain might subside during exercise but that is not necessarily a good thing. It will merely inflame it further, potentially resulting in the onset of chronic tendonitis.

>> **Shin splints:** Like runner's knee, nobody can provide a definitive cause for shin splints. They can occur anywhere along or around the shinbone and cause an ache or a pain that remains constant throughout exercise.

>> **Swimmer's shoulder:** A lot of novice long-distance triathlon competitors experience swimmer's shoulder purely because of the strain being placed on their upper body due to the increase in distances in the pool.

Obviously, the RICE technique is merely the start-point of injury prevention. As stated above, if the injury persists or gets worse, go and see a specialist. They will look at the injury from the perspective of what you have been doing and exactly where the pain is. However, it is always worth trying out the RICE technique first. Many triathletes have frittered away quite a few pounds on physio appointments, only to be told to rest and ice their injury.

If you find that you are picking up repeated injuries on the run then it is always worth going to a running shop and getting your gait tested. Running shoes come in a variety of styles, and most of them these days are designed to compensate for imbalances or issues pertaining to your technique. Make sure you're wearing a pair of trainers that are right for you.

The same can be said with the bike. Because of the number of hours you're going to be spending in the saddle, if you are having problems (most commonly with the lower back or between the shoulders), get your bike fit checked out. It's amazing what difference a slight change in saddle height or a different stem can have on your overall comfort.

MASSAGES

Because of the amount of strain you're putting your body under, giving it a little bit of TLC is certainly not going to do it any harm.

A sports massage can provide many benefits when training for long-distance triathlons. For starters, a sports masseuse can help iron out any niggles or injuries that you are experiencing; they can assess your stretching techniques and possibly suggest improvements; and they can help re-energise muscles that are tight and tired.

A lot of athletes will incorporate massages as part of their training schedule. The simple fact is that tired and tight muscles do not work as well as muscles that are flexible and loose.

CHAPTER 015:
BEYOND PHYSICAL PREPARATION_

'Halfway through the marathon out in the Ironman you meet yourself. There is no hiding from or cheating yourself in this sport. You are stripped bare for all the world to see. It's at that terrible, painful moment you find out what you are made of. When everything hurts so much you want to quit ... you discover your soul. You are free. You are there because you choose to be. You are there because your desire overcomes your fear. You dare to fail ... and sometimes do, but you know that you will be back ... you like the person you meet.'

– Amanda McKenzie, Professional Ironman Triathlete

IF LONG-DISTANCE TRIATHLONS were simply a case of doing the training and turning up for the race, then they wouldn't be so difficult. Unfortunately, they're not. Because training for – and racing – a long-distance triathlon goes way beyond the physical challenge involved.

There is also the need to purchase and maintain the right equipment, the organisation that goes into making sure you are there on race day, and the mental challenge.

Some of these factors are easier to broach than others. Logistics, for instance, we deal with in Chapter 16 and equipment buying is outlined in Chapter 3. If, after reading both of these chapters, you are still running around in a ten-year-old pair of shoes or you think you'll leave the booking of hotels etc. for another day, then good luck to you.

What we're focusing on here and now is the mental approach to long-distance triathlon. How you can master your head so that you prepare properly, train well, get to the race in peak condition, compete and cross the finishing line.

Probably the most common reason why aspiring long-distance triathletes do not show up on the day of a race is due to one thing: burnout. People start off with the best intentions. They train hard, sticking rigidly to their training blocks for the first couple of months. Then the lethargy kicks in. They start to miss their social lives. The novelty of getting up for the 6 a.m. ride wears off. Long-distance triathlon stops being fun. It's another 'thing'; it's a bit like work. But it has a bigger impact on their lives than work. It sends them to sleep at 10 p.m., it tolerates few social excursions, it is everything. And so they stop. They stop training and they stop competing.

Now, there's nothing wrong with that. Long-distance triathlon isn't for everyone. In fact, it isn't for most people. But it's a simple fact that too many people start out with the best intentions and fail, and that is where this chapter comes in.

WHAT IS YOUR MOTIVATION?

This is probably the single most important question you will have to answer again and again about long-distance triathlon: Why do you want to do it? Why do you want to hurt yourself like this? Why? And the simple fact is that only you know the answer. And you do have an answer. Whatever that answer is, that is your motivation.

Hold on to it. Because when it's pouring down with rain and you've been cycling on your own for five hours, that's when you need to remember it. When it's 6 a.m. and cold outside and your body aches but you know you need to swim, that's when you need to remember it. And when you've run for two and a half hours under a hot sun and you can hear your heart beating in your ears, that's when you need to remember it.

Remember it. Hold on to it. And use it to your advantage. Because that is the motivation that will get you to the finishing line of your first, third or even thirtieth long-distance triathlon. Knowing *why* you are doing it is absolutely essential.

Identify Your Major Goal

This is as important as motivation. Simply completing a long-distance triathlon is a goal in itself. But perhaps you want to take it a step further? Maybe you want to set yourself a target time? Maybe you want to set target times for each individual leg?

If you have little experience of competing in triathlons (and more specifically middle- or long-distance triathlons), setting time targets can be difficult. But it is by no means impossible. After some training you should be able to figure out roughly how quick you want to go. But be realistic. There is nothing worse than watching your time slip by on race day.

Once you know what your goal is, write it down and stick it somewhere visible. This is a simple process, but can act as a powerful visual reminder about what you are trying to achieve.

Set Monthly Goals

If you are only aiming at one thing, say, a race in six months' time – the mid-point of your training period can be quite a challenging affair. If, however, you set yourself monthly goals and aim to complete a middle-distance triathlon (or similar goal) a few months out from your race, then you have real, definable goals to aim for.

Training goals are equally important, helping you to stay motivated as you prepare for your first long-distance triathlon. Setting a goal of doing a 100-mile ride three months from the start of your training plan is something specific you can aim for. Running two hours non-stop after two months is something else. Set a goal of swimming 2.5km by the end of month one. These are just examples of the kind of things you can use throughout the training process to help keep your overall motivation intact. There is nothing like seeing some progression in your training to keep you going.

DEALING WITH BURNOUT

The first thing we need to do is define burnout. Burnout is not feeling tired. Nor is it waking up one morning and

thinking 'I can't be bothered'. No, burnout is a feeling of morbid dissatisfaction with what you are trying to do. It's waking up every morning and not wanting to train. It's a complete and utter loss of motivation that grows over a period of time. It is a string of sessions where you can't see any point in what you are doing. Do not confuse burnout for tiredness or having an off day, it is a very different beast.

People get burnout for a lot of reasons. But probably the most common is pacing yourself through the long period of training. UK long-distance athlete Scott Neyedli sums up the problem well; 'If the Ironman is your long-term goal, a strategic build-up of volume over a long period of time is often neglected. I think a big mistake that a lot of triathlon newcomers make is to go out at the start of the season and do ballistic miles and then suffer from burnout maybe 6–8 weeks out from Ironman from when they should be in good or better shape.'

He's correct. Motivation is something that won't be a problem at the beginning of your training. But when you have a spell of hard sessions, or if the weather is bad, it is easy for motivation to drop off. Often, you get to a point when you simply don't want to train at all. It is very common (even the pros talk about it), and happens to the majority of people.

If and when that happens, the first thing to do is take a break. Stop doing – and thinking about – triathlon. Instead, do something completely different. We're not talking about a lengthy spell off, but take a weekend away from the sport. Spend it with your friends or family, go and do what you want to do. But don't train, and don't feel guilty about it. In all honesty, a few days off will probably do you a lot of good.

When you decide you're ready to train again, try a couple of training sessions just for fun. That is, after all, why you started down this path. Get on your bike and just go for a ride. Forget about tempo sessions, interval sessions, heart rates etc. Just go and enjoy cycling. It's the same with running and swimming. Just go and do them because you like doing them (if you're training for a long-distance triathlon, it's a safe assumption to make that you do enjoy at least a couple of the sports involved).

If that's still not helping you get back on track, then take a broader overview of your training. Are you doing too many hours? Are you getting enough sleep? Are you trying to balance too many things in your life? Sometimes, we can become so engrossed in our triathlon lives that we forget to pay attention to other (probably more) important aspects of our day-to-day existences. Take a step back and make sure you are giving enough attention to the things that matter. By that we mean family, friends, work, and yourself (you don't have to spend all of your free time 'doing' things; sometimes you can watch TV or read a book as well!).

If you feel all of that is in order, are you eating properly? With the amount of training you are doing you really need to think seriously about your energy levels. Make sure you are taking enough of the right food and drink on board (see Chapter 13).

Finally, look back at the smaller goals. Have you set them for yourself? Do you have a race to look forward to? There's nothing like a race to get the competitive juices flowing and your motivation back. Even if you are not prepared to go fast, just being part of something can be inspiring. Look out for a short triathlon or a half marathon; you may even surprise yourself!

What is essential to bear in mind is that you are not the only person who feels like this. Most long-distance triathletes go through tough spells when nothing feels like it is going right. Don't be hard on yourself. Accept that you are juggling a lot of balls in the air by taking on this challenge, and it's not surprising if you have a wobble from time to time. It's what you do with that wobble that counts.

VISUALISATION

It's not uncommon when you're out cycling on a lonely road to visualise yourself in the race. Sometimes you see yourself sweeping past Crowie, Macca or Chrissie (Craig Alexander, Chris McCormack and Chrissie Wellington – Ironman World Champions) on your way to an unprecedented victory. At other times, you see yourself breaking through that pain barrier and reaching nirvana on the other side (if you find it, can you tell us what it's like).

Visualisation is a vivid run-through of events in your mind as they may happen, helping you prepare for the task ahead. It's a powerful tool. Everyone is different, but for many they can be really clear experiences and

can be extremely useful in race situations. For example, prior to a race it is not uncommon to see triathletes visualising their transitions. Having that almost unconscious awareness of what you are doing – and the ability to pre-think any problems that may arise – will help you deal with every possible scenario.

Another example is visualising a really positive experience, which often comes if you are performing really well in a training session. Sometimes when running, you feel like you're flying and can keep pushing without getting tired. Recalling positive experiences like this during the race can give a real lift, particularly during the marathon.

DURING THE RACE

If you've put in the hours, days, weeks and months of training, you already know that long-distance triathlons take you on a rollercoaster of emotions. Well, if you can take everything you've felt in the previous five or six months and bundle them into one intense, draining day then you have the race. It is the rollercoaster. From pre-race nerves, to panic in the swim, to ecstatic highs as you head out on the bike, to depression as the kilometres tick by, to positivity, to despair and then finally (and hopefully) to ecstasy and relief at the finish line!

Throughout all of this, the key is to stay focused. Always keep one eye on your goals and the other on your heart rate or level of effort. That will help you maintain concentration, and keep inside the zones at which you know by now you can – and should – be operating.

Long-distance triathlon hurts and you will undoubtedly go through some bad patches and suffer a lot. This is when it gets easy to give up or slow down. If you don't you will regret it. You need to be mentally tough and keep pushing through when things get hard, it's a slightly cheesy saying but in this instance true, 'pain is temporary, glory is forever'.

PART 05:
THE RACE_

>> **CHAPTER 016:**
LOGISTICS_

'The line between disorder and order lies in logistics...'

Sun Tzu, Ancient Chinese Military General, Strategist and Philosopher

OK, SO YOU'VE paid for your entry spot and you've got your confirmation email. Now all you've got to focus on is training, right? Unfortunately not.

Because there are a few logistical considerations that go into competing – and completing – your first long-distance race. And what's more, you need to get some of them done as soon as possible to avoid paying a premium on things.

FINDING YOUR HOTEL

Hotel rooms book up quickly for race day, and so it is essential that you do not leave it too late before sorting out some accommodation. The key thing when looking for a hotel room is location (and, of course, cost). Most race websites will have a list of local hotels, but most tourist offices will also cater for competitors and can recommend accommodation close to the swim start.

And that is where you want to be. The last thing you want is to be driving for an hour (or worse, walking for an hour) just to get yourself down to the start. If you book early, you stand a much better chance of getting a hotel room that is close to the start (and that isn't ridiculously expensive).

If you are competing at one of the more exotic race destinations, you might also want to check out what the local hotel restaurant is like (and what kind of food it serves). You want access to food you are used to eating

during training. After all, you don't want all your hard work to be derailed by a dodgy belly (although sometimes that cannot be avoided). Make sure they serve things like pasta, just to make your life a little easier. Many hotels will also provide a race breakfast from 4 a.m. on race day, which can save hassle, ask the hotel before booking if they plan to accommodate this.

BOOKING A FLIGHT

Unless you live in an obscure area or are making a longer holiday out of the race, the chances are you won't be the only person booked onto a flight to your race destination. Again, book early. Seat prices go up, and more importantly bike spaces get booked out. Unless you are going to pay for someone to take your bike for you (see below), you need to have it on the plane.

The safest thing to do is to book it on the plane (some airlines charge for bikes, but at least you have the peace of mind that it is on there). Some carriers (British Airways and Virgin are two examples at the time of writing) allow you to take bikes for free. If you are flying with them, it is always safest to call them when you have booked your ticket and let them know that you intend to take your bike. They should make a record of that on your booking. That (hopefully) means that your bike has a guaranteed slot on the plane even if 200 other competitors turn up with bike boxes.

TRANSPORTING YOUR BIKE

If you are driving to the race, or you're racing locally, then (again) this section isn't for you. If you are racing abroad, it is.

How you transport your bike is a key consideration. After all, your bike is your pride and joy, and the last thing you want is for it to get damaged en route. You have two options when it comes to bike transportation: do it yourself or pay someone to do it for you. If you are keen to go down the latter route, there are numerous companies out there who will gladly help you, and usually there are race partners that will offer some kind of discount for this service.

If you are transporting it yourself, you need to get either a bike bag or box.

Bike bags are cheaper than boxes, but are obviously less sturdy. You can beef them up with a cardboard bike delivery box (all bike shops have them and will usually give them away for free) and/or some foam. Plumbing insulation tubing is also good for protecting the forks and frame. And always make sure you put something shockproof around your rear mech in case the baggage handler doesn't give your bag the TLC it really deserves.

Bike boxes are a different matter. If you buy one then your bike will be most likely be fine. Before you buy one, check whether your bike fits, particularly if it has a fixed seat post. You can rent them from some shops, too. If you aren't sure how much travelling you are going to do with your bike, look into box rental.

PRE-RACE LOGISTICS

OK, so you've got your hotel, your bike is over and looking good, you've got a few butterflies but, for the most part, you are ready to race.

The Village

The first thing to do is to get settled in. Unpack, put your bike together, run through your kit and then head down to the race village. Most long-distance triathlons will have a race village, and it is basically a large marketplace for kit and the place where you normally

register. If you've forgotten something, don't panic: at worst you should be able to buy something very similar there. You can also get your bike serviced, get a massage and spend a lot of money on various bits of memorabilia.

Check Out The Course

If you can, give yourself an opportunity to check out the course. After all, if you know what to expect, the race immediately becomes less daunting.

Ideally you'll be able to swim, cycle and run various bits of it. However, if you don't have time to do all of this, driving the course and walking parts of the run can really help.

The key when you do this is to pick up on the little things. Examples might be an easily identifiable landmark 400m from the end of the swim so you know when it is coming to an end; the first 20–30km of the bike course so you know what kind of riding to expect at the start of the ride; or the halfway point on the run to help keep your motivation up.

Check Out The Weather

Unfortunately, you can't always guarantee that it's going to be wind-free and mild on the day of the race. With that in mind, check out the weather when you get to the venue. Is it going to be hot, wet or humid?

Just like any long training session, you have to know what the weather is going to do so you can take the kit that you need to compete to your best ability. After all, if you go out in a sleeveless tee and it starts to pelt it down with rain 10km into the bike race, not only are you going to be very wet, cold and miserable, but you probably won't race as well as if you had remembered to take a waterproof layer.

Registration

The day before the race, things step up a gear.

For a start, you have to register. Usually you will need a form of ID (often your passport) and your confirmation email. You will be given your timing chip, race numbers, swim cap, stickers for your bike, helmet and race bags (we deal with all of these in the next chapter), security armband that will get your bike in and out of security, and a variety of assorted paraphernalia that

accompanies triathlon registration. You'll often get a little 'present' as well.

Next step is to rack your bike. This usually starts by joining a queue and then going through a security detail at which your armband is checked against the numbered sticker on your bike. At some races they will also take a picture of you with your bike and provide a security chip that must be fastened to the top tube. This is all so that your bike will be completely safe overnight. Next your bike's brakes and headset will be checked as well as your helmet.

As per most triathlons you then need to locate your racking space and go through the process of working out how you will find your bike following transition and subsequently how to get to the bike exit as quickly as possible. If it's a hot day, it might be worth letting some pressure out of your tyres to ensure there are no untimely tube bursts. (See Chapter 17 for further details and advice on how to rack your bike.)

It makes sense to try and tie your registration in around the race briefing. Race briefings are compulsory for all athletes, and they're good for getting the morale going. In the briefing, the race organisers will run through the main race rules, information about aid stations, and generally try to get you prepared for the race itself. They're an essential part of the race, and the rules of every race are not the same. So make sure you go.

You might then want to check out the pasta party, where you can load up on any extra carbs that you might want (be careful with this) and meet some of the other competitors.

Sign Up For An Early Breakfast

Most hotels in a town hosting a large long-distance triathlon event will do a pre-race breakfast that will begin at something like 4 a.m. However, you might need to sign up for it. It's a good idea and they usually have everything you need (what's more, it's one less thing to worry about).

Getting To The Start Line

This is the final logistical concern pre-race. How are you going to get to the start line? Hopefully you will have booked your hotel just after you secured your entry spot and you'll be a stone's throw from the swim start. If you're not, the best thing to do is talk to your hotel. A lot of races lay on buses for athletes that depart at appointed times from selected locations/ hotels. Just check whether you need to book yourself onto the bus.

If there are no buses and you don't fancy the walk to the swim start, then it's time to book a taxi. Bear in mind that you probably won't be the only person doing that, though, so the sooner you book the taxi, the more likely you are to get it at the time that you want.

Post-Race

The race is run, your legs ache, your stomach feels unnatural, and you're a little bit light-headed. Hopefully you've had a fantastic race, an amazing experience and surpassed your expectations. For the sake of post-race logistics, we'll just assume that you have!

What's more, we're going to assume that you've heeded our advice and given yourself a day after the race to recover before heading home.

The cut-off party

If you're up for it, it is always worth heading down to the finish line to enjoy the finishers' party. The cut-off for most long-distance triathlons is midnight, 17 hours after the normal race start of 7 a.m., and it is amazing how many athletes are still out on the course in the minutes leading up to this cut-off.

If you can, go down and cheer them on. Most of the crowd will have long since departed, and the late finishers need just as much support as you did.

The finishers' party

Just as the pasta party signals the beginning of proceedings, the finishers' party signals the end. A little bit like the pasta party (but with a lot more

alcohol), this is your chance to share stories, see other athletes, and soak up every last ounce of the experience.

Prizes are also awarded to the professionals and age group athletes and it can be a chance to mingle with some of the top professionals and hear their race stories.

The day after

If you are doing an Ironman event, the next day is normally when they announce who has qualified for the Ironman World Championship in Kona, Hawaii for the professionals and age groupers. Those who qualify have to be present with $550 USD (correct for 2010) in cash (or sometimes local currency equivalent) and some ID to claim their place. If qualifiers are not present or do not wish to claim their place, then the place becomes available for the next finisher in the age group and so on (this is called the roll-down) until all the places are claimed. This roll-down of places can sometimes continue way down the finishers' list, so if you have managed a high placing it is always worth attending, just in case.

>> CHAPTER 017:
TRANSITION_

'The price of success is hard work, dedication to the job at hand, and the determination that whether we win or lose, we have applied the best of ourselves to the task at hand.'

– Vince Lombardi, Former American Football Coach

THERE ARE NUMEROUS variables that will affect your race besides the question of how fast you can swim, cycle, or run. Some of them you can't control (the weather, mechanical problems, punctures etc.), some of them you can.

Transition is one of those variables that you definitely can control.

The fourth discipline of triathlon, for many athletes transition is often little more than an afterthought in a race. It is a necessary evil that simply impedes the movement from swim-to-bike or bike-to-run.

But transition in a long-distance triathlon is so much more than a necessary evil. It's a game changer. Forget something basic and your race can turn on its head – 180km on the bike can quite easily become a nightmare if you forget your bike shorts, and a marathon beneath a relentless sun can end up in the medical tent if you don't take your hat or use suncream.

That is why you have to approach the transition for long-distance triathlons in almost the same way that you approach the training: be methodical, make sure you have covered every aspect of it, and go into it knowing exactly what you need to be doing.

PRE-RACE

Your Race Pack

When you register at your race, you'll be given a big pack that contains a lot of items. Some of them are important; some of them are little more than marketing blurb that belongs in the bin. The key is not to throw anything away until you get back to your hotel (or home) and can make sure that you're not sticking something important in the bin.

In particular, you need to look out for:

>> Transition bags

>> Number stickers

>> Timing chip

>> Race numbers

>> Velcro ankle strap for timing chip

>> Race information booklet

The first thing to do (once you're settled) is to put the stickers on your bike, helmet and transition bags if necessary. There are always instructions on where they should go and how they should be fixed. Race organisers are quite particular about this so it's best to pay heed to these instructions.

The Transition Bags

Next up are your transition bags. Because of the sheer number of people competing in most long-distance events, transition is slightly different from that of a standard-distance triathlon.

Instead of having everything piled up around your bike (as in a standard-distance triathlon), you will usually be given three bags. One is for the swim-to-bike transition, one for the bike-to-run and one for the kit you are wearing immediately pre-race (trainers, tracksuit etc.) and will need immediately post-race. The transition bags are hung up on rails in number order and collected before entering the transition tent to change. One of the main reasons for getting your transitions organised is that everything you need for the race must be in these bags, including your helmet,

as nothing can be left by your bike in the racking area (except your cycling shoes, which may be left clipped on to the pedals of your bike if that is your preference).

There are numerous ways of organising what you are going to take, but one of the easiest is to write a list of everything you need for the bike and the run (in particular). Once you have that list, you can tick things off as you pack them. As a guide, most people will need some or all of the items from the following list:

>> **T1 – Swim-to-Bike:** Towel, socks, helmet, cycling shoes (if not leaving them on the pedals), bike shorts, cycle top (if you are not wearing a triathlon suit), gloves, sunglasses, number belt (with number attached), suncream, gels, bars, any other foodstuffs that are not already on the bike.

>> **T2 – Bike-to-Run:** Change of socks, hat, running shoes, change of top, suncream, gels and other nutrition, nutrition belt.

This list is not definitive. There are obviously things you might need to add, and there are also things that you can take off. For instance, not everyone will change their socks or tops in T2, nor for that matter will everyone wear bike shorts or gloves on the bike leg. But remember this transition is not like a standard- or even like many middle-distance transitions. You are going to be spending a lot of time in these clothes and will probably do a fair bit of hurting in them too. With that in mind, a few seconds spent making yourself a little bit more comfortable in transition could actually translate into minutes saved towards the latter stages of the race.

And don't forget suncream! You're going to be out on that course for a long time and in a lot of these races the sun is pretty relentless. You'll be in enough pain the day after the race without having to contend with sunburn.

Lay all of the things you want to take into transition out on the bed. Run through it, double and triple check it, and then pack your transition bags (with a mind to having the things that you need first – a towel for after

the swim, for instance – nearer to the top). Don't forget to do the basics (have your shoes either tied or untied – whichever you prefer), and make absolutely sure you have everything you need.

Finally, it doesn't do any harm to mark your bag with fluorescent tape or something easily identifiable. There are rows and rows of identical bags in long-distance races, and it's not always easy to find your bag and your number. A simple piece of tape – or something that you can pick out when your mind is blurred – can save a couple of minutes of searching. If the weather looks like rain it can also be smart to tie the top of the transition bags for when they are left overnight, to try and keep everything as dry as possible.

You will be allowed access to your transition bags on race day, so if you discover that you've forgotten

something crucial, it isn't the end of the world. But for all intents and purposes, you should go into the bike racking with everything you need in those bags.

Racking Your Bike

Bike racking at a long-distance event is always a somewhat nerve-wracking experience. Not only does it really hammer home what you are about to take on, but you also see some really high-spec kit that is worth taking a minute or two to get envious over. Go and look (don't touch) at the pro bikes, see how they set up their machines and see if there is anything you can learn from the tricks people use, such as taping individual gels to their frames.

However, before you get to the racking stage of the bike, you need to get through security.

Bike racking at most long-distance triathlon events is a very structured, very specific affair. You will be given a time to rack (don't leave it until the last minute as there is invariably a queue) and when you do, many races will usually attach a chip to your bike, take a photo of you with your bike, and give you a wristband with your bike number on it too. Needless to say, non-competitors are not allowed in the racking area.

The reason behind this level of security is simple: there are a lot of expensive bikes in there and nobody wants someone else to be walking off with their pride and joy.

In your welcome pack, there will also be instructions on the procedure for removing your bike from the racking area after the race. Read them and take note of them because they are usually even more stringent than the procedures for accessing the area.

Along with the security checks someone will check your bike is in a safe condition to ride and usually you will be required to take your helmet along too.

In the racking area, you will have a specific place to rack your bike based on your race number. Find your spot, note any landmarks that will help you to identify where you are, and place your bike with the front wheel facing out for an easier exit.

Depending on the race, you may or may not be allowed to place a cover over your bike during the night. At the very least, however, you should be allowed to stick a plastic bag over the seat to stop it from getting damp overnight.

The final thing to do is let some of the air out of your tyres. Not everyone does this, but the idea is that leaving tyres pumped up to race pressure on a hot day can lead to further expansion and possibly a blow-out. You will be able to access your bike in the morning to pump up the tyres, organise your water bottles and nutrition and make sure everything is as it should be.

Placing Your Bags

Like your bike, you will have a specific place to put your swim-to-bike bag and bike-to-run bag, based on number order and usually on a rail of hooks. The first thing you will notice about this space is how small it is. What's more, there's a lot of stuff to put in that bag which means everyone is jostling for what amounts to a very small space indeed.

Unfortunately, there's not an awful lot you can do about it. It's highly unlikely anyone is going to tamper with your bag, but you do need to make sure it is secure just in case any kit is accidentally tipped out. Tie an easily undoable knot in the top of it and place it on your hook.

Like the bike, you will have access to it in the morning.

THE MORNING OF THE RACE

Like any triathlon you've ever done, transition on the morning of the race is a hive of activity. The queue for the toilets is almost as bad as the smell, and people are running anywhere and everywhere trying to fix problems and get ready.

And like any triathlon, the key is to remain calm. There are always bike mechanics around if something goes really wrong, and you have time to do one final check of everything.

The first thing to do is sort out your hydration and nutrition on the bike. Pump up the tyres, check everything is working and get to a point where you are sure that you have done as much as you can.

Next up are your swim-to-bike and bike-to-run bags. Just check them, make sure they're still there and run an eye over everything that is in them. Hopefully you don't need to add anything to them and they're exactly as they were when you left them.

Finally, get changed into your race kit. Place your clothes into the official change bags and take them to the drop-off area. That is it. You're done. You're ready to race. Now just start to focus, take on any last-minute

hydration and get ready for one of the biggest sporting days of your life.

THE RACE

T1: Swim-to-Bike

T1 is always tough. There are always a lot of people milling around and your head is always slightly fuzzy after spending so much time horizontal (and suddenly changing to vertical).

Grab your bag and head inside the changing tent. The great thing about most long-distance races is that there are people to help you through transition. If they're not all busy with other people, volunteers will help you out of your wetsuit and maybe even into the clothes you're wearing for the bike.

Let them help you (it's what they're there for).

Be methodical in T1. Of course, it goes without saying that you shouldn't dawdle, but make sure everything is right. If you hurry through it you might forget something that could make the world of difference when you're hitting the wall at 150km. Be methodical, be precise, but be quick.

And don't get naked. There is generally no nudity in any of the transition zones unless you use the gender-specific change tents. Spare everyone's blushes (and an early disqualification) and keep at least some of your clothes on.

Once you have your clothes on, number belt attached (with number on the back), helmet, gloves, sunglasses, suncream on and nutrition sorted and your wetsuit is back in the bag, then go. Find your bike and head out for 180km.

T2: Bike-to-Run

As bewildering as T1, T2 presents its own challenges. The chances are that there will be fewer people when you arrive in T2, but equally you will be a lot more tired.

First, rack your bike and find your bike-to-run bag.

There will be volunteers on hand to help you take your bike shoes off and sort your kit out. Again, let them help. Obviously, you're going to need to tighten your own shoelaces and put your own suncream on (although sometimes volunteers will help do this as well), but they can help unpack and re-pack your bags.

Again, be methodical – but fast – through transition. Remember: you're about to run a marathon so you want to be as comfortable as you can be. Make sure your hat is on properly and you've applied some more suncream. Also ensure your nutrition is safely stored and won't bounce out when you start running.

If you are feeling completely fatigued or slightly light-headed, take a couple of minutes in T2 just to get yourself back together. As with any aspect of transition, a few seconds lost checking that you have everything you need and that you feel comfortable and ready to take on the next leg can save you minutes further down the road.

Finally, if you are ready to head out again, it's time to hit the road!

POST-RACE

Collecting Your Change Bag

Exhausted, and light-headed but over the moon – you've done it!

One of the first things a lot of people want to do after the race is to change out of their sticky, sweaty clothes. After you've collected your medal, certificate and finishers' T-shirt, you are free to do just that.

Collecting your change bag is remarkably simple. Most people simply stumble up, show their race number and race wristband and your clothes are handed back.

Bike Checkout

Unlike your change bag, bike checkout is a little more arduous, but that's only because they're making sure that people don't walk off with the wrong bike.

You can usually collect your bike on the day of the race, and always the morning after the race. You need to keep your race wristband on (that's very important), and then they will guide you through the process. Usually the process is a simple ID check, making sure they can match you to the photo they took of you with your bike, and then they take away your wristband. It's all for security and it's all to protect your pride and joy. With that in mind, if it takes a few minutes, don't worry about it.

Finally ... relax. You're done. It's done. And the whole thing is a fantastic achievement.

VOLUNTEERS ARE THERE TO HELP

No long-distance event would be complete without the volunteers. They are an essential cog in the wheel of the race, and spend anything up to 17 hours making sure that you have the race of your life.

With that in mind, be nice to them. Yes, you might be exhausted. And yes, you might be in real physical pain. But always remember that they're out there to help you. They're out there to make sure you get what you want when you need it. And what's more, they're doing it for the love of the sport.

If someone isn't around to help you remove your wetsuit, don't shout at the nearest volunteer. If they don't have the right nutrition or hydration at some point, it's not their fault. Like you, they're trying their hardest to help you get to the end of the race. Respect that and respect them.

>> **CHAPTER 018:**
THE RACE_

'When things aren't comfortable, when they aren't 100% going your way, that's the challenge of sport. You have to find a way to adapt and to improvise. If game plan A isn't working, go to game plan B.'

– Craig Alexander, Two-Time Ironman World Champion

THIS IS YOUR time. This is what all of the months of soul-searching and sacrifice are about. Look around you. Everyone is focused. Focused on the hours to come. They are going to be tough. There will be times out there that you will have to dig deeper and push harder than maybe you've ever had to before. Equally, there will be times that you will never forget because they make you feel great (admittedly, most of those are towards the end of the race). But right now you have to focus. And you have to remember: ignore all of the doubts and the negativity – you have done enough training to earn your place on this start line.

THE RACE IN YOUR HEAD

Your body is ready, now you just need to make sure that your mind is focused. Over the course of the day, your head can be both your best friend and your worst enemy.

Your goal is to stay focused and stay positive. Very few people go through a long-distance race and feel mentally on top of things for the whole race. But when

you are feeling down, when your body is hurting, when your mind is telling you to stop, remember: keep giving it your best because if you give up you will regret it.

It's going to be a long day. But if you let your head get the better of you, it will be even longer. When your head is telling you that you've run out of energy, think: by the time you've processed that information you've cycled another 30 metres or taken five steps on the run. So you *can* do it. Just stay focused and stay positive.

AID STATIONS

These are crucial if you're going to complete the race. The distance between aid stations varies depending on the race, but the maximum gap should be 40km on the bike and 3km on the run. If you have to, use every one of them.

Bike feed stations are set into zones. There will be a zone for bananas, one for gels, a zone for water, energy drinks and so on. When you get to the feed station, just shout for what you want. People will direct you and try

and make sure you get it. Remember, though, these guys are volunteers. They are doing their best to help you have the best race that you can. If you miss something or drop something, don't blame them. Equally, don't fly through the station and expect them to be able to run alongside you: they're human, too. The best approach at the bike food station is to slow down (being mindful of your fellow competitors) and make sure you get everything you want. A few seconds spent at a food station could ultimately save you hours if you run out of energy.

The run aid stations are a bit easier to negotiate. They have everything you need for the run (gels, water, Coke, sweets, fruit, pretzels etc.) and volunteers will happily run with you to make sure it doesn't disrupt your race. But be clever: by the time you hit the run, your body is going to be shattered and craving energy. For the first few aid stations, don't be afraid to walk them and make sure you take on everything you need. Better that than run out of gas.

THE SWIM (CUT-OFF TIME: 2:20 FROM THE START)

Whether you are starting on a beach, in the sea or in a lake, long-distance triathlon swims all share one thing in common: they are incredibly demanding. The 3.8km is often the least of your worries.

Like any triathlon swim, as soon as the cannon goes off the water becomes a heaving mass of humanity. You are going to get kicked and pushed and dunked. Accept that.

However, you can limit the physicality of the event somewhat by being in the correct position on the start line. Some races have one mass start; others divide

If things are getting really bad, flip over onto your back or do some breaststroke to get your breath. This should help you to calm down a bit. If it's just unpleasant, tough it out. Eventually the field does string out and it gets easier. Concentrate on maintaining your technique as best you can, and make sure you keep sighting.

The distance shouldn't be too much of a problem – you have done it in training. Keep going, maintain your technique and don't relax into a gentle training plod: always remember that you are in a race.

THE BIKE (CUT-OFF TIME 10:30 FROM THE START)

The bike leg is very long, it's physically demanding, and it takes its toll on you mentally. To sum up the ride as a whole is nigh on impossible. Instead, it makes sense to break the bike leg down into phases.

But before we do that, it's important to make a note on drafting. Because of the number of cyclists on the course, there is an increasing problem with age groupers (and pros, for that matter) gaining time by drafting on the bike. Don't do it. Long-distance triathlons are supposed to be a tough, individual pursuit. If you draft then not only are you belittling the magnitude of the achievement, but you've cheated yourself (and don't deserve to be wearing a medal at the end of the race). Most race rules state that cyclists have to keep right at all times, and that there must be four bike-lengths (approximately seven metres) between you and the person ahead of you. There should be draft-busters all over the triathlon course, and they can hand out everything from four-minute penalties to outright disqualification.

Phase One: 0–60km

Too much of the race can be dictated by the first third of the bike ride. Go off too hard and you may well bonk horribly in the latter stages (leaving you with the small matter of a marathon to negotiate). Don't go hard enough and any time expectations will quickly fall by the wayside.

competitors into slower and faster categories. Be honest with yourself: if you are a 1:20 swimmer, don't go into the faster group. Similarly, don't go into the slower group if you are faster – it might give you clear water for a few minutes, but eventually you'll hit the rest of the field. If it's one mass start, be sensible: hang back or to the sides if you are slower. If you don't, all that will happen is that people will swim straight over the top of you. The basic truths of triathlon swimming hold true in a long-distance race, it's just that there are more people in the water at the same time.

Because of the distance involved and the number of athletes competing, quite often the 'rough' patch of the swim is longer than in a shorter distance triathlon. Sure, you get the inevitable crowd at the start, and you have to wade through the swimmers who went off too fast after a few hundred metres, but you can sometimes expect up to a mile of constant rough water, which can be quite disorientating and, at times, unpleasant.

The thing to remember here is to not get caught up in somebody else's race.

Unless you are a super-fast (or super-slow) swimmer, the chances are you'll be starting the bike alongside a lot of other people. Some of them will start flying down the road; others will take a more sedate approach. You have to concentrate on cycling at your speed. By now, you should have a good idea of what is comfortable, and you should know your legs and heart well enough to know if they are pushing either too hard or not hard enough. Listen to them. Keep your heart rate in the zone and focus on the road.

Targeting other cyclists always helps, too. Everyone has their name on their number and you'll become familiar with a lot of different-named-bottoms on the cycle leg. Either get into the habit of picking people off, or start to cycle 'with' people who are going at a similar pace to you. Other competitors are a great way of

making you keep pace – just remember not to get too close! However, regardless of what the other competitors are doing, watch your heart rate and listen to your legs; they have to get *you* through this race, not the person in the Lycra ahead of you.

There is a note about aid stations following the breakdown of each of these splits, but from the start of the bike these are key. Remember: you're in this for the long haul and you have to keep your body fuelled to make sure you get through it. Take it easy through the aid stations (being mindful of the cyclists around you) and make sure you get the nutrition and hydration that you need. In the early stages of the bike, bananas are a great staple energy source, and bars provide good long-term energy. But be careful: you're going to be consuming a lot of synthetic stuff today, so while you need to keep hydrated, don't go OTT in the early stages.

Phase Two: 60–120km

OK, so you're a third of the way in and have found your rhythm. What's more, you are hopefully maintaining a solid pace that keeps you on track for your target time. Most long-distance bike courses are two- or three-loop affairs, so if you haven't completed the first loop by this stage, you will have done so very soon.

As you pass the midway point in the race, the temptation is to start second-guessing the course: you remember where things were and start expecting them to appear. Whether those things are aid stations, areas where you know your supporters are, or just a hill of note, your mind starts focusing on what is coming. It's difficult not to do so, but it doesn't help you. Things are invariably further away than you think they are, and your mind can make a hill seem a lot steeper and longer than it really is. Instead, try and keep concentrated on your

heart rate monitor and bike computer. You still have a very long way to go and the hardest part is yet to come, so make sure you maintain that focus.

It's at this stage in the race that you need to get your nutrition and hydration right. You're about to come to the toughest part of the bike leg and you want to go into it as strong as possible. Make sure you are drinking plenty of liquids – and not just energy drinks. Just like on a training ride you may get sugar cravings at this point. All food stations hand out Coke and don't be afraid to take some. But always make sure you have two well-stocked bottles on your bike. You don't want to be running out of liquids now. And keep the food coming. Keep the bananas coming, and continue taking gels or have another bar.

Phase Three: 120–180km

This is where the training miles kick in. Yes, it hurts. Yes, you want to throw your bike in a hedge. And yes, you still have a good hour or two of cycling to go. But dig deep. Your legs are going to hurt and your mind will start playing tricks on you. It's natural. But that hill that you flew up on lap one isn't as big as you suddenly think it is. And no, the crowds aren't dwindling. You are simply (and quite understandably) tired.

And you are also nearly there.

This is where staying positive is key. Keep focused and grind it out. A lot of people find the 140–150km stretch a tough one as there is still another hour-and-a-bit of cycling to go. But rationalise it: you have less than 40km left – that's an Olympic distance triathlon. You eat those for breakfast.

Speaking of eating, keep doing it. Keep your mind on the bike, but have half an eye on the run. It's coming, and you want to be fuelled and ready for it. With 40km to go, the last bar should be eaten and now you're looking at gels (and maybe a banana). You want to have enough in the stomach to keep you fuelled, but not so much as to leave you retching on the run. If your body is craving sugar, give it sugar. You know yourself well enough now.

You'll know when you have about 10km to go. You'll know, because the familiar landmarks will be etched into your mind (and maybe for a very long time afterwards) and all of a sudden you won't feel as exhausted. Don't go too hard these last 10km, but don't ease off. As with the rest of the bike, monitor your heart rate and stay within your zone. Take a gel in time for the run and make sure you are hydrated. Oh, and hang on to those water bottles – they're nice little souvenirs!

THE RUN (CUT-OFF TIME: 17:00 FROM THE START)

For a lot of very fit (and probably incredibly sane) people, a marathon is about as much exercise as they will ever do on any given day. For you, it will (hopefully) be a shorter leg than the one you have just completed.

There's no two ways of saying it: this marathon is going to be tough. But, like the bike, that is why you have to break it down into manageable chunks. Look at it as a marathon and it is a very long way. Look at it as 4 x 10km runs (ticking off each 10km as you go) and it's definitely achievable.

What's more, there will be plenty of people along the way cheering you on. Whereas at times the bike can feel quite lonely, there are spectators along much of a run course and they're usually impressively vocal. So enjoy it!

Phase One: The First 10km

Like any triathlon, the first few kilometres of the marathon are simply a case of battling through the dead feeling in your legs. Just fight it for those first few kilometres. Have confidence in the fact that you will find your rhythm and you will eventually start to run as normally as anyone who has just cycled 180km can run.

Watch your heart rate. If it shoots through the roof, ease off a bit. Get it under control. You need to keep your heart rate in the zone to have any chance of posting a decent time on this split, so make sure you do that.

And keep fuelling. In a lot of races there will be food stations every 2km. If you feel like you need to, walk through the early food stations. They have gels, fruit, drinks, and – if it's really hot – sponges. Use the sponges to keep you cool and take on the food and drink you want. Don't just hammer the gels though. Sooner or later your stomach will simply stop accepting them and that can spell trouble. Maintain a mix of the synthetic and the natural.

Phase Two: The Second 10km

OK, you're a quarter of the way through the run and, although it hurts, you've finally found your stride. The key here is to try and focus on technique. You breeze through 20km on a training run and by the time you knock off this 10km you're pretty much halfway.

We'll say it again: keep eating and drinking. You have to. You may not want to but your body needs it. Mix it up and take on what you need. If you're struggling, pause at the food stations and just make sure you take on exactly what you want. It is better to take an extra minute at a food station to get your fuelling right than to run out of energy altogether during the latter stages of the marathon.

Phase Three: The Third 10km

Dig deep. Grind it out. Yes, it hurts. Yes, you probably want to stop. But you're more than halfway there. What's more, if you're on a two-loop course, you now know exactly where you'll be running and on what kind of terrain.

This is where mental strength comes in. Unless you're of the 'pain is good' mindset, this is the time to really focus on maintaining a positive mental attitude.

Remember why you're doing this and how far you've come. The distance left to run is relatively trifling compared to the miles that you've already raced.

This phase of the race is a classic time for things to start unravelling. People really do hit the wall and it can be really tough to force your way through it. You'll see it happening all around you as people fail to deal with the heat or simply run out of energy. Don't let that happen to you. Keep hydrated. Keep fuelled. And keep going.

Phase Four: The Final 10km

OK, you have one eye on the watch, the other on the road. Everything really hurts now. But you're nearly there. If you were fresh you would be finished in well under the hour. It doesn't matter that you're not. The key thing here is that you know you can run this 10km. You know it because you've done it over and over again.

Can you still hit your target time? What sort of pace should you be running to do it? Focus on that – you don't want to miss your target by a couple of minutes because you let your mind wander at this point.

Stay positive.

If you dug deep around 30km, now is the time to dig really deep. You have to be tough. Every sinew of your body might be telling you to stop, but by the time you've processed that thought you've already run another five paces. If you can, switch your head off. It can be a destructive force when it comes to this stage of the race. Focus on something – anything – but not the thoughts milling around inside your mind. You can carry on and you will carry on. It just hurts a little bit – that's all.

Hydration and fuelling are trickier now. A lot of people find that they simply cannot take on any more synthetic foodstuffs. You might even start having stomach cramps or feel a bit nauseous. It's understandable; your body has been consuming unnatural things pretty much solidly now for at least eight hours. Try and keep fuelling but don't make yourself sick. If you really can't stomach any more sticky, sweet things, try some fruit or even just plain water. You need to try and keep the energy coming just because your body needs something.

Phase Five: The Last 2.2km

The last couple of kilometres. The toughest part of the race is arguably run, but this is by no means easy. Look at your watch – how close are you to hitting your target time? Is it going to be tight? Get a move on then. Has it slipped by? Who cares! Pick a time and run under that.

Can your legs do it? Don't give them a choice – make them. After all of this time, they can deal with another ten or fifteen minutes of pain. Just push. It's almost over.

The Finish

Unless you're perilously close to missing your target time, enjoy this bit of the race: you've earned it. If you have the time, say hello to your family and friends (it's a very long – and emotionally draining – day for a spectator as well). High-five people on the course. Make the most of the fanfare at the finish.

Sometimes there are cheerleaders. Quite often there are grand stands full of people cheering you on. This is your time and you really do deserve the attention and the applause: you've just done something that 99 per cent of the planet can't do. And at no stage is it easy.

If you're close to your target time, then by all means go hard down the finishing straight. If not, don't gazump a fellow competitor by out-sprinting them at the finish. Let them have their moment just as you want to have yours. This is a moment that you (and they) will treasure for the rest of your life.

POST-RACE

The chances are that at some point in the hour or so following the race you are going to feel a bit funny. Not everyone does. But some people feel light-headed, others sick, and some just simply pass out.

Immediately after receiving your medal, someone should be on hand to check you are OK. If you are feeling at all unwell (and not just utterly exhausted), let them help you out. They'll sit you down, wrap you in some silver foil and give you a drink. If you feel *really* unwell, tell someone. The medical tent will be stocked with intravenous drips and beds for recovering on. Plenty of people take advantage of that kind of hospitality at a race, so don't feel embarrassed to do so.

If you're feeling OK, enjoy the moment. Share it with your family and friends and take the obligatory photos.

You then have three choices:

1. Return your timing chip and collect your finisher's T-shirt and certificate.

2. Go and eat something.

3. Get a massage.

The first option is obligatory. Whether you decide to do that first or last is up to you – just make sure you do it (otherwise you'll lose the deposit you placed on the chip).

As for the food vs massage choice, that is down to personal preference. Both, though, are free, and both are advisable.

If your stomach is saturated with gels and bars, try and get something savoury inside you. Remember: your body is still going to be eating away at energy and fat reserves long after you have finished so you need to be putting stuff back in. Maybe you don't want to, but you really need to. It could be anything from plain bread to chocolate ice cream; just give yourself some food.

A massage is a particularly good idea if you don't feel like stretching after the race. If you do nothing, your body is going to be horrifically stiff for three or four days after the event. If you have a stretch or get a massage, you'll still feel a bit stiff (which is natural), but you should be able to stand and walk without looking like you've been shot in the leg.

After that? Go home, have a bath, answer a million text messages from people all desperate to find out how you went, and feel really proud of yourself.

THE 17-HOUR CUT-OFF

Who are the most celebrated athletes at most long-distance events? Well, the winners, obviously. But the people who come in around the 17-hour mark run them pretty close.

There is always an amazing atmosphere at the end of many races.

If you have the energy and the desire, go down and cheer home the last few athletes out on the course. Some of them will not make it in time. Others will sneak in just under the 17-hour mark.

And for those that do, there is a rapturous reception. Often the winners will be on hand to give them their medals. It's not uncommon to see Mexican waves and cheerleaders dancing to the music as they make their way through the night and up to the finish line. And as the 17-hour cut-off passes, event organisers will usually put on a firework display and have a party for everyone who has stuck it out. It's well worth a visit, if not simply to marvel at the energy that some of the slower competitors possess at the end of the race.

>> POSTSCRIPT_

SO IS IT WORTH the effort? Well, only you can decide that. But one thing we can say with some certainty: you won't ever forget your first long-distance triathlon. Whether you smashed your target time, were smashed by the race, or everything simply went to plan, there will be memories and experiences from the last six months that will live with you forever.

Sometimes it's hard to grasp what you have done straight after the race. Sometimes you need days – or even weeks – to get your head around the emotional and physical investment you have made over the last six months. Give it time: the race is done now.

This is the time to start planning. Planning how you're going to make up for all those hours you haven't seen your friends, family or anyone else. Planning what you're going to do with all the spare hours you suddenly find yourself with in the week (not to mention abundant energy levels).

Maybe it'll be time to plan your next race. Despite the fact you may have stumbled across the line in a bleary haze of pain and euphoria and swore that you would never do another long-distance triathlon ever again, never say never. You see, triathlon – especially the long-distance variety – is horribly addictive. And once you've analysed your splits and the dull ache in your legs fades away, you know that you can go quicker. And it would be a shame to waste all that training when it's pretty easy to keep your body ticking over, wouldn't it?

Of course, nobody is holding a gun to your head and saying 'do another one'. There are plenty of people out there who have a go and decide it's not for them. The important thing is that they had a go. Whatever you decide to do now, whether you walk away or jump right in, you can always be safe in the knowledge that you had a crack at it.

But, of course, you haven't just taken away an exceptional level of physical fitness from the last six months. The physicality of the race is just one small part. Yes, you've grown physically stronger, but you're also mentally stronger too. You have challenged yourself on numerous different levels, showing a total dedication to a very tough pursuit. And because of that you should feel enormously proud.

Completing a long-distance triathlon should give you the confidence to know that you can tackle something big and complete it. You can apply that to every area of your life, and use it to its great advantage. Now is the time to use this and take on your next challenge. Good luck!

>>GLOSSARY_

Age grouper
All those triathletes who aren't professionals are termed age groupers.

Age groups
Triathlon races are often split into age groups who are regarded as your competition for prizes or Kona slots. Age groups typically range from <20, 20–24, 25–29, 30–34, 35–39, 40–44, 45–49 etc.

Bento box
This is a flexible box that is strapped onto both your top tube and handlebar stem. They are useful for storing nutrition.

Bonk
Also known as chucking a whitey, hitting a wall, passing out. It happens when your carbohydrate reserves run out because you haven't fuelled correctly.

Brick session
A brick training session combines more than one discipline, for example a swim followed by a bike or a bike followed by a run.

Carbon fibre
Carbon fibre (polymer or reinforced plastic) is a very strong, very light (and quite expensive!) material used to make middle- to top-end bikes. For the same strength, a carbon fibre frame weighs a lot less than its steel or aluminium equivalent.

Catch
The point in the swimming stroke when swimmers apply pressure to the water to help them move forward.

Check in/registration
The time/place where you need to pick up your race packet (containing number, race chip, swimming hat etc.) and/or take your bike to rack in the transition area.

Cleats
Clip-in pedals require a cycling shoe with a cleat fitted to the sole which locks into the pedal and is removed by twisting the foot.

Clip-in pedals
Designed to accept cycling shoes with a cleat, locking the foot into the pedal and allowing for greater efficiency in the pedal rotation.

Drills
A number of different exercises to improve your swimming stroke or riding stride.

Elites
Also known as the professionals (or the very best age groupers).

Energy gel
A small packet of gel that contains concentrated, syrupy carbohydrate providing a surge of energy.

Intervals
A set number of repetitions run with a rest between each repetition. The rest might be active or a complete stop. Interval training is used to improve speed endurance and work the aerobic system.

Ironman®
Ironman is the original long-distance triathlon, raced in Hawaii. The Ironman brand now covers a number of long-distance and middle-distance races worldwide and is owned by the World Triathlon Corporation (WTC).

Ironman® World Championship
The Ironman World Championship is held in Kona, Hawaii every year. Professionals and age groupers need to qualify from one of the other Ironman races held around the world.

Isotonic drink
An isotonic drink has the same salt concentration as the normal cells of the body and the blood, allowing the replacement of fluid and minerals lost during exercise.

ITB
Illio-tibial band. The muscle that runs up the side of the thigh, from the kneecap up past the hip.

Pronation

The distribution of weight through the foot. You could be a neutral, over- or under-pronator, which should in part determine the running shoes you buy.

Pull-buoy

A swimming float that is held between the (non-kicking) legs to allow full concentration on the arm stroke.

RICE

Rest Ice Compression Elevation – the solution to many common triathlon injuries.

T1

Transition one – swim-to-bike.

T2

Transition two – bike-to-run.

Tempo

A training pace designed to improve your speed endurance.

The fourth discipline

Also known as transition.

Timing chip

Given by race organisers (for a refundable deposit), the chip is wrapped in a velcro band that goes around the ankle. Records your split times as you run/cycle over timing mats.

Track pump

A large pump that can pump up a tube in a small number of pumps and to a high pressure. A worthwhile investment!

Transition

The area where you go to change between the disciplines.

Tri-bars

Also know as aero bars, these can be clipped on to the handlebars of your road bike allowing you to get into a more aerodynamic position. Alternatively you could have a tri-specific bike that has integrated aero bars as part of the bike. These bars have the gear shifters at the end of the bars and more accessible brake levers.

Tri-suit

An all-in-one or separate shorts and top suit, with a shammy in the shorts to aid cycling comfort. Made of fast drying material that wicks sweat from the body. Also designed with rear pockets to carry gels and a long zip to help the body keep cool.

Triathlon wetsuit

A triathlon wetsuit is made of a thinner neoprene than a traditional wetsuit, with more flexibility particularly in the shoulders and arms, allowing easy swim action.

Waves

If a triathlon has a large number of entrants it is often impractical for everyone to start together, so competitors are split into start waves (often by age group or previous finishing times) going off every 15 minutes or so.

>> FURTHER INFORMATION_

WEBSITES

www.triathleteeurope.com

www.ironman.com

www.endurancecorner.com

www.trainingbible.com

www.slowtwitch.com

www.tritalk.co.uk

www.k226.com

MAGAZINES

Triathlete Magazine

Triathlete Europe

Lava Magazine

220 Triathlon

BOOKS

Be Iron Fit: Time-efficient Training Secrets for Ultimate Fitness, Don Fink, The Lyons Press, Guilford, Connecticut, 2010 (2nd edition)

Endurance Sports Nutrition, Suzanne Girard Eberle, Human Kinetics, 2007

Going Long: Training for Triathlon's Ultimate Challenge, Joe Friel and Gordon Byrn, Velopress, Boulder, Colorado, 2009 (2nd edition)

Lore of Running, Tim Noakes, Human Kinetics Europe Ltd, Pudsey, West Yorkshire, 2002

Practical Sports Nutrition, Louise Burke, Human Kinetics, 2007

Racing Weight: How to Get Lean for Peak Performance, Matt Fitzgerald, Velo Press, 2009

Sports Injuries Guide Book, Robert Gotlin, Human Kinetics, 2007

INDEX_